CRICUT MAKER

4 Books In 1

The Most Complete Collection Of Books To Master The Use Of Your Cricut Machine. Discover Countless Project Ideas And Use The Design Space App To Easily Craft Amazing Projects

Christy Cain

TABLE OF CONTENTS

PART 2 CRICUT MACHINE AND ACCESSORIES

PART 3.   CRICUT DESIGN SPACE

PART 4.   CRICUT PROJECT IDEAS

Introduction

With Cricut, anything is possible. If you've been speculating what you can do with your machine, the simple answer is almost anything. For designers, for those who like to make precise cuts, and for those who like to print their own shirts, this is a wonderful option to consider. If you are thinking of getting a Cricut machine, you'll see here that there is a lot that you can do with this unique tool and endless creative possibilities.

Cricut is a home die-cutting machine that can be used for various art or craft work or projects like scrapbooking and textiles.

Most of us, whether we're Cricut pros or a beginner, have seen the many items for sale at craft shows and in specialty stores. Everything from popular saying and quotes stenciled on wood signs to monogrammed water tumblers and most everything in between.

Some Cricut users have mastered the machine, and they can make vinyl letters look as if they were painted onto the wood. The vinyl meshes so well that with the naked eye, you won't be able to find a spot to lift one of the vinyl letters. That's how realistic it can look. And most types of vinyl are weather-resistant. That means you can make all kinds of awesome things for the outside as well as inside.

The Cricut machine is leading to a revolution in paper crafting. It's readily portable and operates without being hooked on a computer so that you only pick this up from the handy carrying handle and proceed. But do not allow the advantage to fool you; this system isn't a toy. It's capable of producing an unlimited range of letters, shapes, and phrases anything you can imagine. There are no limitations!

The Cricut machine comes in handy for anyone—individuals or crafting businesses trying to create beautiful looking pieces of art for personal or commercial use. The Cricut Machine can be simply defined as a professional-looking device used to create papercrafts, gift tags, boxes, ornaments, custom kitchen accessories, towels, crafty/DIY projects, Christmas gifts, interior décor signs, custom T-shirts; and birthday presents.

It offers a high-level cutting performance of up to ten times compared to other cutting machines thanks to its powerful blades—rotary and knife. The machine is commonly referred to as a smart cutter, partly because it uses a precision cutting mechanism, making it ideal for all types of crafts.

PART 1.

CRICUT MAKER
FOR BEGINNERS

Chapter 1.
What Is the Cricut Maker and How to Get Started

The Cricut Maker

The newest Cricut die-cutting machine is the Cricut Maker. If you thought that the Explore Air 2 was a great model, then you should get ready to be blown away.

The Cricut Maker is a rare unit amongst other die-cutting machines. The rotary blade is already enough to attract experienced users. And, for beginners, it provides an avenue for improvement and unlimited creativity

The Cricut Maker is known as the flagship model of Cricut. It's the one that can do almost anything under the sun on almost any material you can bring into your machine's mat guides. The price point is the only drawback of this powerhouse model, and unless you want to make crafts to sell, this model proves to be quite expensive. Either way, you can be confident that whatever you do with this machine will always be of the highest quality. This baby is going to pay for itself in a short time if you sell your crafts.

This machine is full of exciting features for the enthusiastic crafters who want to turn up at the party with the most exquisite creations that are ahead of their colleagues. This model really has everything.

There is no other Cricut machine with the speed of the Cricut Maker. The cuts that can be made using the precise blades that fit this machine are smoother than anything from a straight knife or other craft cutters you could ever expect. You can easily remove the tip from the housing using blade housings, add the next one, clip it back into place and start to roll your designs. Moreover, the machine will identify the loaded material, so at the start of the project, you won't have to specify the type of material. One common problem in the other models is that the project is halfway completed before the crafter discovers that the dial has been set wrongly.

The machine is, as some other models, fully Bluetooth compatible and ten times more powerful than any other with a specialized rotary cutter attachment that allows it to glide effortlessly through fabrics with accuracy.

This year, a new model was released called The Cricut Maker. It has the capability of cutting more materials than any previous models, and the company boasts its fast, precise cutting.

The Cricut Maker is considered to be Cricut's flagship model. This is the one that can do just about anything under the sun on just about any material you can fit into the mat guides of your machine. The one drawback of this powerhouse model is the price point. This does make this model more prohibitive unless you plan to make crafts that you can sell with this model. If this is your intention, you can rest assured that whatever you turn out with this machine will be the best of the best, every single time. If you're selling your crafts, this baby will pay for itself in little to no time at all.

With that in mind, the Cricut Maker costs $399.99. That is a large sum of money for someone who doesn't have it and even for someone who does have it. My advice would be to save until you can afford it or put it on your wish list in the meantime and subtly hint to your loved ones that you'll absolutely love to have one of these bad boys. Hopefully, someone will catch on and not balk at the huge amount of dollars that it will eat up.

The Cricut Maker can be used with your own images, which is a plus for those who prefer to use their own or don't want to buy a subscription or pay for individual images. It allows you to personalize your items and make your own statement. You can make personalized cards, signs, and anything your heart desires. The ability to personalize your items with multiple lines and fonts broadens your horizon, and if you make products to sell, you can offer personalization.

Capability

The Cricut Maker, as an updated version of others, is very powerful and flexible. It comes with a toolkit that includes a rotary blade, knife blade, deep cut blade, and fine point blade. It also comes with a single and a double scoring wheel, as well as a collection of pens. The pens include a fine point pen, a washable fabric pen, a calligraphy pen, and a scoring stylus.

The machine also improves its efficiency by adding some unique features. We have the adaptive tool system, which means that the device can adjust the angle of the blade and the pressure of the blade automatically depending on the material. It doesn't need the Smart dial feature because the Cricut Maker determines your cutting force for you, and its decisions are usually accurate.

It has two clamps, one for the pen or scoring tool and the other for the cutting blade. This system is also unique because of its fast mode and precise mode. This works for any paper, cardstock, and vinyl.

Materials

As expected, the Cricut Maker will be able to handle more and thicker materials than the machines in the Cricut Explore series. From light materials to basswood and leather, this machine will exceed your expectations. Cricut Design Space also provides a lot of benefits for Cricut Maker users/. It allows .jpg, .gif, .png, .svg, .bmp and .dxf files.

The system also supports a wireless Bluetooth adapter. You can also enjoy the Sewing Pattern Library if you own a Cricut Maker. The library contains 50 ready-to-cut projects, and it is a result of a partnership between Cricut and Riley Blake Designs.

Another great benefit you get when using Cricut Maker with Design Space is that you get free membership of Cricut Access for a trial period.

The only downsides to this model are that it is quite slow when working with very thick materials, although that is expected. It also produces a lot of noise because of the fast mode.

How to Get Started

Before plugging in the machine, make sure that you have removed all the safety and travel packaging materials. These include foam around the blade housing, plastic tape strips to keep the compartments closed, and so on.

- Go to www.cricut.com\setup for the step-by-step setup guide to get the machine connected to a device and Design Space.

- Choose "Cricut Maker"

- The first screen will be the 'Welcome to the Cricut Family' screen.

- Click the green 'Get Started' button.

- If you have not as yet set up a Cricut ID, the next screen will prompt for this to be done.

- If you do have a Cricut ID, at the bottom of the screen, there is a "Sign in" button beneath "Already have a Cricut ID?"

- The Cricut ID is required to work in Design Space to be able to create your projects.

- Answer the next screen, which is the 'Getting to know you' screen.

- The next screen is the "Connect machine" step which the program will take you through, step-by-step.

- Make sure that the machine is positioned at least 10" from the wall.

Connecting the Cricut Maker With the USB Cable

Use the USB cable that was provided with the Cricut Maker machine. You can buy these separately, should anything happen to the one that came with the machine. Plug the small square side of the cable into the square USB port located next to the power port at the back of the Cricut Maker.

Plug the larger flat USB part of the cable into the USB port of the computer that will be connecting with the machine.

Plugging in the Maker

Use the power supply that comes with the Cricut Maker. Plug it into the wall socket with the power on the wall socket turned off.

Plug the other end into the power socket on the Cricut Maker, switch on the wall socket, then power up the Cricut Maker by pressing the power button.

Cricut Maker Firmware Update

When the machine syncs up with and is found by the software, the next screen will check the firmware version of the machine. The firmware contains updated drivers, features, commands, and so on.

There will be a section that will let you know what the current version is and what version is on the Cricut Maker. It is advisable to update the firmware if the machine's firmware is not the same but older than the currently available firmware version.

When you update the firmware, the power button on the Cricut will change to red, and the load/unload mat button will turn white. There will be a progress bar to show how far the update download is. The Cricut Maker will automatically reboot upon completion of the firmware update.

This section will also automatically register the Cricut Maker machine.

Click "Continue" to take you to the next setup section.

Chapter 2.
Differences Between Cricut Maker and Explore Air 2

Cricut Maker & Cricut Explore Air 2

Both have a very similar physical appearance, but the big difference is the cutting power that each one has and the adaptive tool system that only the Cricut Maker has, allowing you to change the blade without having to change the casing.

The Cricut Explore Air 2 allows you to cut more than 100 types of materials from cardboard to vinyl, but it has a cutting force of 400gr, a much lower figure than that of the Maker. It lets you cut materials up to 2.4mm thick thanks to its 4kg cutting force.

What does this mean? That the Cricut Maker allows you to cut many more materials such as balsa wood, chipboard, leather, etc. It has a special blade to cut thicker materials; it is the Knife Blade. Thanks to its gear system, it allows greater control of cutting tools, being able to cut materials with greater precision and force.

The Explore Air 2 has a dial on the machine itself where you can select the material you are going to cut, or you can put it in «Custom» to choose the material from Design Space. Instead, in Maker, you choose it directly from the application.

The Cricut Maker has a much broader tool pack than the Explore, such as the Scoring Wheel that allows you to perform much more precise marking, the engraving knife, the wave knife, the drilling knife, and the debossing knife.

Plus, it lets you cut fabric with the rotary blade that's already included in the Cricut Maker box without the need to purchase the stabilized fabric blade as you need for the Explore.

What conclusion do we draw with all this? If your projects are based on vinyl or thin cardboard, the Cricut Explore Air 2 is the best solution, but if you want to go a little further, definitely buy the Cricut Maker.

When the Cricut Maker was introduced to the public in the summer of 2017, one of the buzzing questions was; how does it compare to the Cricut Explore Air 2?

It's a valid question because the Cricut Explore 2 (a fantastic machine) had just been released also and is, by all standards, a fantastic cutting machine.

The truth is that both are excellent stand-alone machines that are extremely efficient at what they are designed for. However, there are pros and cons associated with both, and each crafter will be more suited to either one.

The bout between the Cricut Maker and the Explore Air 2 is on, and this is an opportunity for you to closely examine the right choice of cutter for you.

Some Comparisons

Versatility

In terms of versatility, there's only one winner—The Cricut Maker!

The Cricut machine does 100% of what the Explore Air 2 can do, and even more. It consists of an adaptive tool system that can cut over 100 different materials and a huge library of sewing patterns. When you consider all this, you'll realize that the Cricut Maker is versatile enough to work with a variety of tools—including all types of blades released by

Circuit, the brand new Knife and Rotary blades, and yet to be released ones also. You don't have to look any further because the Rotary blade that comes with the Cricut Maker during purchase already puts it above the Explore Air 2.

The blade needs no supporting or backing material because it easily cuts through all types of fabric.

In theory, the Explore Air 2 is capable of cutting fabric but not as good as the Maker. Thus, a backing material is always required because the fine blade often catches on the fabric. Furthermore, users of the Explore Air 2 machine always use separate fabric cutters to get their desired cuts, but in contrast, a Maker is an all-purpose machine that does it all.

Cutting Specs

When we talk about cutting specs, we are referring to the machine that cuts best. Besides, cutting is the reason why people even go out to buy the machine in the first place.

If you consider the price (entry-level price) of the Cricut Explore Air 2, you'll agree with me that it is extremely cost-effective. The machine remains one of the best cutters around because its German-made carbide blade cuts through materials with extreme ease, and that's why it is used to make designs that are small and intricate.

In contrast, the Cricut Maker comes with blades that aren't only sharp and precise but also possess a lot more force behind them; the Cricut Maker has about 4,000 grams of force, whereas the Explore Air comes with a paltry 400 grams only.

The Cricut Maker cuts easier and neater; it requires fewer passes on thicker materials and can work with way more materials than the Explore Air.

Furthermore, the Maker is designed to potentially work with newer and sophisticated blades (such as the Knife blade and Rotary blade), as opposed to the Explore Air.

In terms of fabric cutting, the Rotary blade remains a revolutionary invention that has greatly improved the industry; however, the Knife blade has proven to be safer and more effective—It is the ultimate tool for cutting thick materials.

The Explore Air 2 is a highly efficient cutting machine that is perfectly suited for crafters that stick to thin materials and do not require any special intervention.

The maximum cutting size of both machines is 12" wide by 24" long, and most industry experts are of the view that the Maker's cut size should have been increased to at least the size of the Silhouette Cameo 3 (12" wide by 10" long).

Price $$

It is obvious that the Cricut Maker is an improved version of the Explore Air 2; however, many people are of the view that those improved features fail to justify the hike in price.

The Cricut Maker is listed at $399.99 on the Cricut website, and although it comes with improved features, many people see it as a significant amount to lay down on a cutter. On the other hand, the Explore Air 2 is listed at $299.99, and during sales, the price drops down significantly.

Longevity

Generally, when people weigh their options for products they intend to purchase, most of the time, they consider price ahead of other factors, but the truth is that price isn't everything. Thus, another factor to look out for is the products' longevity.

In terms of longevity, the Cricut Maker and the Explore Air 2 are very solid machines, and there's absolutely no doubt about their durability. However, the Maker seems to be more suited for the future because the cutter will ultimately outlive the one of the Explore Air 2.

Besides, the Cricut Maker comes with the Adaptive Tool System, meaning that it is guaranteed that it'll be compatible with all types of blades and tools that will be released in the foreseeable future.

No matter how much the crafting process evolves over the next couple of years, the Cricut Maker will remain effective and relevant.

On the other hand, the Explore Air 2 is not designed to offer more than it already does, and although it won't become obsolete, it just can't support the newer blades and tools that are being released by Cricut.

In comparison, the Explore Air 2 is meant for people that are happy with their available options and concerned about upgrading their skills, whereas the Cricut Maker is suitable for people that intend to experiment and develop their crafts further.

Software

In terms of software, there's nothing that separates these two machines because they both use the Cricut Design Space software.

Design Space Software is a decent program that is easy to use and contains plenty of editing options for users to effectively personalize their designs. Besides, there's a store that contains hundreds of editing options for users to use and personalize their designs.

Users can upload their designs and convert them free of charge; thus, expert users can create their complex designs in more sophisticated programs like Adobe Illustrator, Corel Draw, Make the Cut, and Sure Cuts A Lot.

Cricut Design Space is cloud-based, so users can design on their personal computers, tablets, and phones. It is a user-friendly program, but it has its flaws: sometimes it gets buggy and limiting, especially while creating new designs within the program.

Sewing Projects

In terms of the usage for sewing projects, it's a no contest! The Explore Air 2 is a versatile machine, but it doesn't measure up to the Cricut Maker. On the other hand, apart from the actual Sewing Machine, the Cricut Maker is what people use for serious sewing projects. The Maker comes with a library that contains plenty of sewing patterns, and not only will it cut the sewing patterns, it also marks them with the washable fabric marker pen. The Cricut Maker eliminates guesswork with regards to the marking of patterns, and this ultimately improves the final output of the work.

Portability

One of the most important but often overlooked features of machines is portability. If you're a crafter that prefers to be static, then you can overlook it, but if you're someone who prefers to travel with your cutting machine, then you have to consider the size of the machine.

Between the two machines, the Cricut Maker is heaviest, weighing almost 24lbs as against the Explore Air 2 that weighs only 14.8lbs The Cricut Maker is a static machine specifically designed for use in a specialized space, home, or craft room. It has plenty of storage space and even comes with a provision for charging phones and/or tablets.

The Explore Air 2 is nimble, and it comes with a smaller amount of storage. Thus, it is perfect for people that like to craft on the road.

In terms of portability and ease of movement, the Explore Air 2 stands taller than the Cricut Maker.

Ease of Use

Both machines are relatively easy to use with little practice, but in terms of ease of use, the Cricut Maker edges the Explore Air 2.

The Explore Air 2 is built with the Smart Set Dial on the front, and this allows users to easily select from the most common materials. Once the dial is set, the machine automatically adjusts its cut settings accordingly.

However, the problem faced by most users is that most of the materials that most cutters use are not always the most common materials for members of the larger Cricut community. Thus, you have to manually set the material settings from within Design Space if your material isn't on the dial. It is not an extremely difficult process, but it is a bit frustrating, especially when you have to carry out the same procedure over and over again.

On the other hand, the Cricut Maker automatically adjusts its settings according to the type of material that is loaded on the cutting mat. It is extremely easy, and the user doesn't have to do any settings at all.

Cartridges

Newcomers in the world of Cricut and the cutting of crafts might not understand this; however, long-time Cricut users will know all about the cartridges—they might even have a space dedicated to them in their craft rooms.

It is no longer mandatory to use cartridges for designs on both the Cricut Maker and the Explore Air 2. However, in case you have a couple of old cartridges at home, you might want to use them; thus, you can plug them directly into the Explore Air 2 and use them. It is possible to use the cartridges with the Cricut Maker, but it is a bit more complex. You will have to get the cartridge adapter that will allow you to link the physical cartridges into Design Space. The cartridge adapter uses a USB port to connect the Cartridges with the Maker.

There is also the option of using digital cartridges instead of buying the adapter. The digital cartridges are downloaded directly into Design Space.

Print Then Cut

The last and final battle between the Explorer Air 2 and the Cricut Maker is which of the machines has better performance for Print Then Cut.

The Cricut Maker comes with the Print Then Cut (PtC) feature, which allows users to print out their designs onto white paper and then cut.

This feature comes in handy for crafters that tend to experiment more on new designs, as opposed to just downloading designs from Cricut Design Space.

The Explore Air 2 also has the same PtC feature as the Cricut maker; however, the difference is that the Cricut Maker can PtC on colored and patterned paper, while the Explore Air 2 cannot. Thus, in terms of Print Then Cut, the Cricut Maker edges the Explore air 2.

At this point, it is obvious that the Circuit Maker is the superior machine. It is more durable, offers better Print Then Cut functionality, easier to use, more versatile, and an all-around better cutter.

The Explore Air 2 is a very good machine that has served crafters for some time now and will continue to do in the future; however, the Cricut Maker is just too good for it. The Explore Air is the perfect machine for crafters that use paper, thin materials, cartridges, and also those that have a limited budget.

Both machines are highly efficient, and they serve their purposes perfectly; the Cricut Maker is for makers, while the Explore Air 2 is for cutting crafters.

Chapter 3.
Tools and Accessories to Get Started

Basic Tools in Cricut Maker

Cricut machines can also be used with a ton of tools, and most of them are pretty straightforward to use. Here are some of the best tools to consider for your machine:

- **Wavy tool:** Helps you cut waves into your design.

- **Perforation tool:** Helps to make perforated markings in your design.

- **Weeding tool:** This is one of the best tools to use when working with vinyl because it helps with peeling vinyl from the backing sheets.

- **Scraping tool:** This helps remove any tiny pieces off of the design and prevents the material from moving around.

- **Spatula:** This is a great one because it helps with moving the design off the backing without tearing the material and can keep it free of debris.

- **Tweezers:** These are good for pulling the tiny pieces of vinyl or other design elements from the middle without pulling the edges or tearing them.

- **Scissors:** Cricut scissors are durable, made of stainless steel with micro-tip blades —perfect for detailed work.

- **Paper trimmer:** This is really convenient with straight cuts, so you do not need to use scissors or a ruler. It is essential for working with vinyl.

- **Brayer:** If you are using fabric or larger pieces of vinyl, this is actually one of the best tools to keep the material stabilized on your mat, so the mat itself is not damaged.

- **Backup mats:** This should be obvious, but if you are going to work with larger projects, the carpets do lose their stickiness after a while. This can prevent you from having to leave your project to pick up more.

- **EasyPress Tool:** This is awesome for iron-on vinyl that you do not want to iron. It also holds the vinyl much better, even if you wear it a lot, and eliminates the temperature and time guesswork you may otherwise have to do. It is a little pricey, but there are beginner options.

- **Brightpad:** Finally, you have a Brightpad, which helps make the lines that you need to cut more visible. If you are doing more than just one cut, this is handy since it will help with tracing and with adapting the patterns, too.

These tools are essential, and to pick up the first few on the list, you will want to get the toolset since it is much cheaper. But if you are going to be using your machine a lot, I highly recommend spending a little extra by picking up tools to use with

Latest Tools for Cricut Maker

Cricut has just announced four new tools for Cricut Maker. As we already knew, one of the advantages of the Maker is what they called the "Adaptive Tool System," which promised to develop a lot of new tools to use with the machine. And so it is being.

The first thing to keep in mind is that the four new tools that are going to be released will be mounted on the Quick Swap Housing, or "Quick Change Bracket," which is the same bracket that the scoring wheel uses. If you have the scoring wheel, you will know that changing the head is as easy as changing a blade, so there are no complications. Therefore, you can use all the new tools with single support and, if you already have the scoring wheel, you will not need to buy another one.

Debossing Tip

This is what we normally call "embossing tip," but it is actually called "debossing" because "embossing" is the relief up and "debossing" is down. In this case, since the tip is going to press on the paper, it will make the relief to the bottom and, therefore, it is called a debossing instead of an embossing tip.

The advantage of these tips is that when using them in our cutting plotter, we can make a totally personalized design. Unlike other systems like the Big Shot, which work with folders, in this case, we will have total freedom of design. We will have to see how the finish is. Emboss always works best on soft or thick surfaces, so it will be an ideal match for foil cardstock, thick papers, feather board, and even balsa wood!

Engraving Tip

Finally, they have taken out the metal engraving tip that we have been waiting for so long. With this tip, we can engrave on metal plates. With the strength of the Maker, we can likely record on something more than aluminum or tin, but it will still have to be seen in operation to know it. On the other hand, it can also be used on other materials such as wood, methacrylate, plastic, or leather. It is ideal for making pet tags, engraving key chains, creating commemorative plaques, and many more things that we are sure will come up with.

Chapter 4.
The Different Types of Blades and Their Functions

Rotary Fabric Blade

The rotating fabric blade is capable of cutting with extreme precision. All Cricut blades that work with the gear system are very efficient at making perfect cuts. This blade is ideal for cutting varied fabrics, felt and soft, less dense materials such as cork.

It should be used with the fabric cutting base (pink) because this base is more resistant and suitable for the way the Rotary Blade works. Regardless of the material you are cutting, use the pink base!

Avoid cutting pieces smaller than 2 cm. Its way of working would end up spoiling the cut by turning it to cut something so small. This blade works only with the body made for it, but its blade can be changed when worn out—just like all other Cricut blades. The Rotary Blade is for Maker's exclusive use and comes with the equipment but can also be purchased separately.

Materials you can cut with the rotating fabric blade:

- Fabrics in general (silk, chiffon, even jeans)

- Synthetic, mixed, and cotton

- Fabrics with Lycra

- Jute, smooth velvet, and corduroy

- Crepe paper

- Cork

- Felt national and imported—without treatment!

And do you want a sensational tip that almost nobody knows? You can cut up to three layers of cotton at once with the Rotary Blade! That's right; you can triple your production. There is a whole technique to be followed, but it is possible!

Deep Cutting Blade (Knife Blade)

This is an extra-deep blade with great cutting power. It cuts dense and thick materials up to 2.4mm. Its strength and precision are incredible, and it is ideal for cuts with moderate detail. The deep cutting blade does not fit in another body, but, like the other cutting blades, you can only change the tip when it wears.

The Adaptative Tool System ™ is exclusive to Maker and developed to work together with gear blades, as it allows movements that cause the material to be cut in all directions. And this guarantees the complete cut of thick and dense material, such as the 2mm chipboard, for example.

Materials you can cut with this blade:

- Chipboard

- Balsa and Bass Wood—similar low-density woods

- Soft materials, but over 1.7mm—which is the limit of the Prod undo

- Paspatur or Passe-partout cutting blade—that is the material used around a framed image.

Drilling Blade

One of the advantages of the adaptive tool system is the ability to use rotary blades. Until now, we had the normal rotary knife, but now two new models will arrive. First, the drill, or dotted line, what this blade does is cut broken lines and leave bonding points on the paper, the typical dotted line that is then used to break. This is very practical for making tickets and packaging that can later be opened. Considering that Cricut Design Space did not give us the option of cutting dotted lines, this new tool is a great advance when it comes to making designs.

It is necessary to say that they will be 2.5mm cut lines and 0.5mm uncut holes as a technical detail. Perfect for throwing later and cutting into a lot of materials—paper, cardboard, rubber, acetate.

Wave Blade

Another typical model of circular blades is wave cutting. In this way, we achieve a different finish on our cuts with minimal effort. The wave knife will turn our straight lines into a subtle zigzag, and that can come in handy, for example, when creating a card edge or giving a different finish to any project. I remind you that these two heads, although they are rotating blades, will not be mounted on the support of the rotating blade but on that of the scoring wheel.

Materials That Can Be Worked on Using a Cricut Machine

When you look at what Cricut makers can do, you're going to realize there are a ton of materials to choose from. But, which ones do you really need? Which ones are kind of useless? Well, here are some of the main materials you should consider buying and the materials that you don't necessarily need when using your Cricut machine.

Iron-On Vinyl and Adhesive Vinyl

This is one of the best materials for a Cricut blade, especially fine-point Cricut blades. You can adjust the settings and design the image onto the vinyl. Then, by ironing it on or using the Cricut press, you can design shirts and other appliques for outfits; however, you'll want to make sure that the iron-on setting is on your Cricut before you think about using this.

You will realize that when you start to look for vinyl, the ideal type to choose is heat-transfer vinyl since you can simply iron or press it on. There are many different options, including fuzzy locked or glitter vinyl, that you can purchase.

Adhesive vinyl is another good one, and there are many different ways to use this— Containers, ornaments, and the like benefit immensely from this material. You can get permanent outdoor and removable indoor options. Again, Cricut machines are known for cutting vinyl, and this material is worth it if you're thinking about making decals, as well.

Cardstock

If you're doing any scrapbooking or making cards, you'll want to consider crafting your items with cardstock. You can choose some great 65-pound cardstock for your crafting projects, and the nice part about this option is that it's pretty cheap.

Paper

Cereal boxes, construction paper, embossed paper, even freezer paper can be used with your Cricut machine. Some users have had a lot of luck with the poster board, too, but you'll want to make sure you clean your blades if you plan on using this material since the poster board can be quite trying on them. Your blades could end up dulling over time, so make sure you clean them with aluminum foil.

Craft paper is another option, as well, and if you're creating personalized boxes, this is a good material to consider—it can help bring a more personalized touch to your finished product.

Fabric

With some fabrics, you'll need a lighter grip board, such as for silk or polyester, but if you're working with heavy fabrics such as leather, burlap, or canvas, make sure that you have StrongGrip cutting boards. But the fabric is another great option for your Cricut experience since they are wonderful for cutting fabrics, and fabrics can also be printed on. You will want to make sure you use a stabilizer, such as Heat N Bond or Wonder Under before you cut them to prevent the fabric from getting messed up. Different cuts can be made to fabric and textiles with the Cricut Explore machine. Cricut maker machines work best with fabric, though there is the consideration that it could be a bit pricey.

Alternative Materials

While those are the main materials, you also have some other alternative options. If you're working with light material, typically, the Explore machines series is ideal.

One great material you could try is the chipboard. If you're working with chipboard thicker than what your blades can handle, then you can insert the material into the Cricut machine and let it work its magic.

Rubber is another option that a lot of people don't think about when they're using a Cricut machine. If you're trying to create custom-designed stamps, such as for pottery or other projects, consider this option. You'll want a deep-cut blade for this, but it works. Wood veneer works well with your Cricut machine, but you'll want to make sure that you have both a fine-point and a deep-point blade, depending on the project. This material will also take a little longer to cut.

What about magnets? That's right; you can actually make your own customized magnets with a Cricut machine. These are great for gifts for teachers or friends, and the best part is you don't have to sit around trying to cut out intricate designs on your own. They're wonderful and super fun.

Craft foam is really good for arts and crafts with children, but if you don't want to spend all your time cutting out various shapes for the kids to use, just insert the design into the Cricut machine and let it do the work. This is wonderful for art teachers who want to put together a project but don't want to deal with the hassle of spending all their time prepping the materials.

Finally, you have a mat board. This will require a deep-point blade, but if you want a strong material for a durable art project, this is a wonderful option.

The craziest part of Cricut machines is that they can cut items you wouldn't ever expect—tissue paper, stencil paper to make your own stencils, sticker paper to make stickers, plastic packages, adhesive foil, and even aluminum foil can be used with this! So, yes, there are so many options for your Cricut experience and so many designs that you can take advantage of that it's worth checking out, that's for sure.

Cricut machines can handle a ton of materials, to put it simply. The general idea is that if the machine can cut it, chances are you can use it, so don't be afraid to try some of your crazy ideas—Cricut machines are quite wonderful for just about everything.

Chapter 5.
Tips and Tricks

Cricut Blades Maintenance and Care

Use Your Blades With Recommended Materials

Your blades' life can be decreased if you are not using your blades properly and as recommended. At the same time, you need to get a hold of which mat to use for which type of material by yourself; as Design Space doesn't recommend appropriate mats, Design Space will help you choose suitable blades based on the material you are using for your crafting project. Moreover, you need to make sure that the right blade is used on the material you are cutting, as you can damage the blade if you choose to cut the wrong type of material. Follow the advice from Design Space and make sure that each of your blades is used on an appropriate material or fabric.

Protect the Blades and Housing Gears

Quick Swap Scoring Wheel and blades for all Cricut machines have plastic covers. Make sure to keep these covers and use them to protect your blades when not in use. By properly storing your blades, you are protecting your tools from outside particles that can compromise the functionality of your tools, such as dust. The plastic cover protects blades and housing gears at the same time.

Store Your Blades Properly

When you are not using your blades, make sure to cover them and store them properly. You can keep your tools in a storage pouch or a box. Blades can be safely kept in your Cricut machine. The machine is designed to provide storage for the blades you are not using, while the storage compartment also has a magnet to keep your blades neatly stored. You can keep your tools in the Cricut machine storage compartment as well. This way, you will always have all the blades and tools you need, accessible whenever you want to use them, but also protected and safe from damage.

Maintaining the Cricut Cutting Mat

You also have to clean and maintain your Cricut cutting mat because that is where the cutting takes place. If the cutting mat isn't clean, it can stain the machine. Also, if your cutting mat has stopped sticking, it can spoil your designs and creations.

When your mat is no longer sticky because of debris and grime, cleaning it and making it sticky again will bring it back to life. The solutions that I will mention are not ideal for the pink cutting mats, only for the green, blue, and purple.

Using Baby Wipes

Make use of alcohol-free, unscented, and bleach-free baby wipes to clean your mat. You should use the plainest baby wipes that you can find so that you don't add lotions, cornstarch, solvents, or oils to your cutting mat. If not, you could affect the stickiness and adhesive of the mat. Also, after cleaning it, let it dry completely before using it.

Using a Sticky Lint Roller

You can also use a roll of masking tape if you don't find a sticky lint roller. Run the roll across the mat to get rid of hairs, fibers, specks of dust, and paper particles.

This form of cleaning can be done daily or between projects so that dust doesn't accumulate on the mat. This is a fast way to remove dirt apart from using tweezers or scrapers.

Using Warm Water With Soap

You can also clean the mat with soap and warm water. You should use the plainest soap possible, too, so that you don't mess with the mat. Use a clean cloth, sponge, soft brush, or a magic eraser. Also, rinse it thoroughly and don't use it until it is completely dry.

Using an Adhesive Remover

In the case of heavy-duty cleaning, then you should use a reliable adhesive remover to clean it properly. When using an adhesive remover, read the directions properly before you start.

Then, spray a little amount on the mat and spread it around with a scraper or anything that can act as a makeshift scraper.

Wait for a few minutes so that the solvent can work on the mat. Then, scrape the dirty adhesive off your mat with a scraper, paper towels, or cloth. After this, wash the mat with warm water and soap in case there is leftover residue and let it dry properly.

How to Make Your Cutting Mat Sticky Again

After washing or cleaning your cutting mat, you have to make them sticky again. The most advisable way to make your mat sticky again is by adding glue to it. Get a solid glue stick like the Zig 2-Way Glue Pen and apply it to the inner portion of the mat. Then, stroke the glue around the mat and ensure that there is no glue residue on the edges of the mat.

After about 30 minutes, the glue will turn clear. If the cutting mat turns out to be too sticky after you apply glue, you can use a piece of fabric to reduce the adhesive by pressing the material on the parts of the mat that are very sticky.

Cover the mat with a clear film cover after a few hours. You can also use tacky glues or spray adhesives that are ideal for cutting mats.

Maintaining the Cricut Cutting Blade

You can use your Cricut fine point blade for over a year if you maintain it properly! The same goes for the other types of cutting blades. When maintaining your Cricut cutting blade, you have to keep it sharp all the time so that it does not get worn out.

Keeping your blade sharp is essential because if it isn't, it can damage your materials and cause wastage. Also, if you don't maintain your blades, you will have to replace them often.

Keeping Your Cutting Blade Sharp

Spread a portion of aluminum foil on a cutting mat. Without removing the blade from the housing, cut out a simple design in the foil. This will sharpen the blade and remove any paper particles, or vinyl stuck on the blade. This can be used for any type of cutting blade.

In the case of heavy-duty cleaning, you should squeeze a sheet of aluminum foil into a ball. You need to remove the blade from the housing of the machine to use this method. Then, depress the plunger, take the blade and stick it into the ball of aluminum foil repeatedly. You can do this 50 times. This will make it sharper and also remove vinyl or paper particles on the blade.

How to Store Your Cutting Blade

The best way to store your cutting blade is to leave it in the Cricut compartment. You can place it in the drop-down door that is in front of the machine. That compartment is meant for storing the blade. As for the blade housing, you can place it on the raised plastic points at the back of the machine. There are magnets in the front of the machine where you can stick loose blades.

When you put your blades in the Cricut machine, you never lose your blades.

Your Machine Is Tearing Your Material

These are some steps to take if your Cricut machine is tearing your material:

- Check if the smart is set on the correct setting and check if you have selected the correct material in the design space.

- Try to verify the size and quality of the image you have cut. If you are cutting an image that is of very high quality, try cutting one free from duplicity.

- Try making use of a new blade and mat.

- After all, these steps have been completed, and the problem still persists, please try contacting assistance care.

Your Fabrics Always Get Caught Under the Rollers

If you are experiencing this problem with your fabrics, check if the fabrics are placed outside the tenacious area of your mat by allowing them to pass under the rubber roller bar. If that happens, the fabrics can be gripped by rubber rollers. It is recommended that you cut down a size that will fit the mat but will not extend outside the tenacious area. The recommended and standard sizes for the tenacious area on the fabric grip mat are 12x24 and 12x12, respectively.

Chapter 6.
Step by Step Projects for Beginners

Leather Cuff Bracelet

Supplies Needed:

- A small piece of leather
- A bracelet or piece of chain or cord, and small jump rings
- Needle-nose pliers for jewelry
- Deep cut blade for the Cricut Explore

Instructions:

1. Your first step is to choose the design image that you would like to use on your leather bracelet. This can be found inside the image files under "Lace" or any other design file that you already have.
2. Next, verify that the sizing is appropriate for a bracelet by cutting it on paper. You definitely do not want to cut the leather and be wrong. This would waste the materials.
3. Once the size is perfect, you can begin your project.
4. Place the leather on the mat with the smooth side down and push the "Cut" button.
5. After the leather piece is cut, you will need to adjust your chain or rope to the appropriate size that is needed for the wrist of the person that it will be fitting.
6. Connect the leather to the chain with the jump rings. Attaching the links to the leather is perfectly fine, but it may tear the leather, so using the jump rings is a great alternative.
7. This is a simple process that anyone with a Cricut and a need to make leather goods can do.

Vinyl Wall Decals

Supplies Needed:

- Adhesive vinyl
- Cricut machine
- Weeding tool
- Scraper tool

Instructions:

1. Log in to the Cricut design space.
2. Create a new project.
3. Click on "Upload Image."
4. Drag the image to the design space.
5. Highlight the image and "Flatten" it.
6. Click on the "Make It" button.
7. Place vinyl on the cutting mat.
8. Custom dial the machine to vinyl.
9. Load the cutting mat into the machine.
10. Push the mat up against the rollers.
11. Cut the design out of the vinyl.
12. Weed out the excess vinyl with a weeding tool.
13. Apply a thin layer of transfer tape on the vinyl.
14. Peel off the backing.
15. Apply the transfer tape on the wall.
16. Smoothen with a scraper tool to let out the air bubbles.
17. Carefully peel off the transfer tape from the wall.

Wooden Hand-Lettered Sign

Supplies Needed:

- Acrylic paint for whatever colors you would like
- Vinyl
- Cricut Explore Air
- Walnut hollow basswood planks
- Transfer Tape
- Scraper
- An SVG file or font that you wish to use
- Pencil
- Eraser

Instructions:

1. You will need to start by deciding what you will want to draw onto the wood. Then, place some lines on the plank to designate the horizontal and vertical axis for the grid. Set this aside for later.
2. Upload the file that you wish to use to the Design Space. Then, cut the file with the proper setting for vinyl.
3. Weed out the writing or design spaces that are not meant to go on the wood.
4. Using the transfer tape, apply the tape to the top of the vinyl and smooth it out. Using the scraper and the corner of the transfer paper, slowly peel the backing off a bit at a time. Do it carefully. Remove the backing of the vinyl pieces, aligning the lettering or design so that it is fully centered. Place it carefully on the wooden plank.
5. Again, use the scraper to smooth out the vinyl on the plank.
6. Take off the transfer tape by smoothing off the bubbles as you scrape along with the wood sign. Discard the transfer tape at that time.Continue to use the scraper to make the vinyl smoother. There should be no bumps since this creates bleeding.

7. Now, paint your wood plank with any color of your choice. Peel the vinyl letters off. Once the paint has completely dried, you can erase your pencil marks.

Cloud Coasters

Supplies Needed:

- Whichever Cricut machine you have chosen to purchase
- An active account for Design Space
- A pair of scissors
- Fusible fleece
- An iron
- A sewing machine
- Cotton fabric and thread to go with it

Instructions:

1. Grab your fabric.
2. Cut your fabric and make sure it is twelve inches.
3. Open your design space and hit your button that says a "New Project."
4. Click on the button that says "Shapes" and then insert a shape that looks like a cloud. You are going to do this from the pop-up window.
5. You will need to resize your cloud to five and a half inches.
6. Click on the button that says "Make It."
7. Change your project copies to four. You will have to do this so that you can have a front and back to each coaster.
8. Click the button that says "Apply."
9. Click the button that says "Continue."
10. Adjust your settings for the materials to medium fabrics (like cotton).
11. Load your mat with the attached fabric.
12. Hit "Cut."
13. Repeat three steps, but you will be placing the fleece on the cutting mat, not the fabric.
14. Change your cloud shape to 5.7.
15. Select a material and click where it says "View More."
16. Then type in "Fusible Fleece."
17. Cut out two of your fleece clouds.

18. Attach one of the fleece clouds to the back of one of the fabric hearts. Use a hot iron.
19. Repeat this step with the second heart.
20. Place your right sides together, and then sew the clouds together. When you do this, make sure that the fleece is attached. Leave a tiny gap in the stitches for turning.
21. You will now need to clip the curves.
22. Turn your cloud so that it is right side out.
23. Press your cloud with the iron.
24. Fold in the edges of your cloud's opening, and then press again.
25. Stitch around your cloud a little bit from the edge. We recommend a quarter of an inch.

You are now done with this project and can give your cute little clouds to someone you care about and brighten their day. The neat thing about this project is that it can go in any shape you wish. You could have so much fun with this by making rainbows, dinosaurs, flags, military ammo; the options are endless, and you can gain great ideas for fabrics and materials to do this project with. It is also a good beginner's project to do because you can get used to different commands on the machine as well.

Cosmetic Bag Designed With Cricut

Supplies Needed:

- Fabric for the outside
- Thread
- 9-inch zipper
- Lining fabric
- Bags bottom fabric
- Cosmetic bag pattern
- Cricut
- Cutting Mat

Instructions:

1. Open your pattern up and cut out the pieces that you will need to make the cosmetic bag. While you are doing this, cut the lining that you will need also.
2. Using the mat, cut the outer fabric and then the inner fabric. Use the "Cotton" setting for the lining.
3. Cut the bag's bottom with sturdy material and choose whichever setting matches the fabric used.
4. If you use the Cricut faux leather, you will have a sturdy bottom that does not cost as much as real leather but is just as sturdy.
5. Place the right sides together and proceed to sew one of the outside panels to the pieces that are used for the bottom. This should leave a 1/8 inch allowance for the seam. This should be the measurement for all seams. Repeat this step with the lining and the bottom. Next, place your zipper face down with the right side of the zipper on the outside of the bag. Then, place the top edge of the lining at the top of the zipper, lying face down. Line your edges perfectly and pin them together.
6. Using a zipper foot that is attached to your sewing machine, sew the zipper close to the teeth. At the end of the pull, stop and place the needle down into the material. Lift your sewing foot up and pull your zipper from the machine past the point that is already sewed. Place the foot back down and continue sewing.

7. Iron this fabric so that it is smooth, and then sew a top stitch on the edge of the fabric. Repeat this step on the other side.

8. Place the outside of the fabric lying face up, and then place the lining face down. Pin these pieces together with your zipper foot, following the same steps you did previously. Iron this side and then proceed to finish the topstitch.

9. Sew your other outside bottom piece and then sew the sides of the lining to the bottom of the lining. Make sure to leave the opening about a few inches wide, so you can turn it inside out later on.

10. Making sure you have the zipper open, proceed to sew the edges of the bag together. This should be the lining end to the bottom of your bag.

11. Proceed to sew the corners and then flatten the unseen edges and center your seams. Sew the piece closed and then repeat the process for the bottom as well as the lining.

12. Trim up all your hanging threads and the parts of the zipper that are sticking past the edge of your fabric bag. Using the unsewn hole, flip the bag right side out and check your work.

13. Sew up your lining hole by folding the raw edge just a bit, making sure to sew close to the edge. Backstitch to make sure the sewing is permanent and trim the ends off.

14. Push your lining into the bag and push your corners out of the bag to properly form the bag. Zip your zipper and admire your work.

Fabric Bookmark

Supplies Needed:

- Using a Design Space file that is designated for the bookmark's size, cut the fabric.

Instructions:

1. Start with placing the fabric on the cutting mat and running it through the Cricut with the appropriate settings.
2. If you are making more than one bookmark, then copy the bookmark onto the Design Space within the parameters of the cutting mat.
3. You will need pieces of fabric per bookmark.
4. Using a Cricut Maker, you can cut more pieces at a faster pace.
5. Cut your interfacing fabric or cardboard into the dimensions of 6.75" h x 0.75" w, with one per bookmark.
6. Attach your fabrics together with the wrong sides facing using some pins. Sew your long sides and the bottom together. Use the foot that is for edgestitch to guide the fabric with a straight line. Sew with the needle down setting to pivot at the end of the corners. Make sure you backstitch the beginnings and ends of the lines.
7. Fold the casing of your bookmark on the right side. Using a pencil, you can push the corners of the bookmark out so that it is right side out. Using your iron, press the casing to flatten.
8. Insert the interfacing fabric that is fusible inside your bookmark.
9. Fold over the top edge and use the iron to press it with the heat.
10. Proceed to sew the top shut.
11. Using the iron, press the bookmark so that it is fused and flat. The heat will fuse the bookmark and interfacing fabric.
12. Now that you are done, you will be able to make bookmarks out of fabric.

Leather Geometric Buffalo Pillow

Supplies Needed:

- Cricut Maker
- Cricut X
- Cardstock Cricut
- Cutting Mat
- Cricut Fine Point Blade Glue or Tape Runner

Instructions:

1. Use the connection above to resize the flowers to the size you need, then click "Make It."
2. Once cut, you can collect any parts you want. I hotly attached my toothpicks to the top of my cake. For the term topper, I used bigger wood skewers to stand above the flowers. Instead of flowers, this would be super sweet with mini paper rosettes.
3. Use paper and your Cricut maker to create custom cake decor. With every addition to the tools the Maker utilizes, the Cricut Maker has already made it so much easier to create the possibilities.

Sugar Skulls With the Cricut

Supplies Needed:

- Printer
- Toothpicks
- Standard cardstock
- x standard grip mat for Cricut
- Sugar skull "Print then Cut" image
- Cricut Explore machine
- Cricut Design space software
- Glue

Instructions:

1. Use your Cricut Design Space; you need to log in.
2. In the Cricut Design Space, you will need to click on "New Project" and then select the image that you would like to use for your sugar skulls. You can use the search bar on the right-hand side at the top to locate the image that you wish to use.
3. Next, click on the image, and click "Insert Image" so that the image is selected.
4. Click on each one of the files that are in the image file and click the button that says "Flatten" at the lower right section of the screen. This will turn the individual pieces into one whole piece. This prevents the cut file from being individual pieces for the image.
5. Now, you want to resize the image so that it is the size that you wish it to be. This can be any size that is within the recommended space for the size of the canvas.
6. If you want duplicates of the image for the sheet of sugar skulls, then you should "Select All" and then edit the image and click "Copy." This will allow you to copy the whole row that you have selected. Once you have copied, you can then edit and paste the multiple images to make a sheet. This is the easiest way to copy and paste the image over and over again.

7. Follow the directions that are on the screen for printing, then cut the sugar skull images.
8. Using glue, piece the front and back of the sugar skull together to create the topper with the toothpick inserted into the center of the pieces.

Pendant With Monogram

Supplies Needed:

- Necklace chain
- Jewelry pliers
- Cricut gold pen
- Cricut Explore Air
- Cricut strong mat grip
- Cricut Faux leather
- Jump ring
- Fabric fusion

Instructions:

1. Start by opening the Cricut Design Space. Choose the size that you want the pendant to be. This can be a circle pendant. Using the machine, make another circular-sized pendant.
2. Attach the jump ring here later after the circles have been made.
3. Next, open the text section in the Design shop, and type in the exact initials that you would like to use.
4. Select the section that has a "writing style" option from the menu and adjust the font of the lettering to whatever you wish.
5. Drag your letter to the center part of the circle and resize it to fit the appropriate size. Be sure to make a front and a back. This will ensure both sides of the piece look like leather.
6. Create your circle so that it matches the other one minus the letter. Make this an attached set.
7. Using the Cricut pen, begin to cut the pieces. As it is cutting the leather, it will print the initials.
8. Use your fabric fusion glue to join the two pieces of leather together, making the pendant.
9. Using the pliers for jewelry, you can twist on the ring for the necklace. Attach your pendant and jump ring together, and then string it onto the chain. The pliers can close the jump ring off.

Paw Print Socks

Supplies Needed:

- Socks
- Heat transfer vinyl
- Cutting mat
- Scrap cardboard
- Weeding tool or pick
- Cricut EasyPress or iron

Instructions:

1. Open Cricut Design Space and create a new project.
2. Select the "Image" button in the lower left-hand corner and search "paw prints."
3. Select the paw prints of your choice and click "Insert."
4. Place the iron-on material on the mat.
5. Send the design to the Cricut.
6. Use the weeding tool or pick to remove excess material.
7. Remove the material from the mat.
8. Fit the scrap cardboard inside of the socks.
9. Place the iron-on material on the bottom of the socks.
10. Use the EasyPress to adhere it to the iron-on material.
11. After cooling, remove the cardboard from the socks.
12. Wear your cute paw print socks!

Night Sky Pillow

Supplies Needed:

- Black, dark blue, or dark purple fabric
- Heat transfer vinyl in gold or silver
- Cutting mat
- Polyester batting
- Weeding tool or pick
- Cricut maker

Instructions:

1. Decide the shape you want for your pillow, and cut two matching shapes out of the fabric.
2. Open Cricut Design Space and create a new project.
3. Select the "Image" button in the lower left-hand corner and search "stars."
4. Select the stars of your choice and click "Insert."
5. Place the iron-on material on the mat.
6. Send the design to the Cricut.
7. Use the weeding tool or pick to remove excess material.
8. Remove the material from the mat.
9. Place the iron-on material on the fabric.
10. Use the EasyPress to adhere it to the iron-on material.
11. Sew the two fabric pieces together, leaving allowance for a seam and a small space open.
12. Fill the pillow with polyester batting through the small open space.
13. Sew the pillow shut.
14. Cuddle up to your starry pillow!

Clutch Purse

Supplies Needed:

- Two fabrics, one for the exterior and one for the interior Fusible fleece
- Fabric cutting mat
- D-ring
- Sew-on snap
- Lace
- Zipper
- Sewing machine
- Fabric scissors
- Keychain or charm of your choice

Instructions:

1. Open Cricut Design Space and create a new project.
2. Select the "Image" button in the lower left-hand corner and search for "essential wallet."
3. Select the essential wallet template and click "Insert."
4. Place the fabric on the mat.
5. Send the design to the Cricut.
6. Remove the fabric from the mat.
7. Attach the fusible fleecing to the wrong side of the exterior fabric.
8. Attach lace to the edges of the exterior fabric.
9. Assemble the D-ring strap.
10. Place the D-ring onto the strap and sew it into place.
11. Fold the pocket pieces wrong side out over the top of the zipper, and sew it into place.
12. Fold the pocket's wrong side in and sew the sides.
13. Sew the snap onto the pocket.
14. Lay the pocket on the right side of the main fabric lining so that the corners of the pocket's bottom are behind the curved edges of the lining fabric. Sew the lining piece to the zipper tape.
15. Fold the lining behind the pocket and iron in place.

16. Sew on the other side of the snap.
17. Trim the zipper so that it's not overhanging the edge.
18. Sew the two pocket layers to the exterior fabric across the bottom.
19. Sew around all of the layers.
20. Trim the edges with fabric scissors.
21. Turn the clutch almost completely inside out and sew the opening to close.
22. Turn the clutch all the way inside out and press the corners into place.
23. Attach your charm or keychain to the zipper.
24. Carry your new clutch wherever you need it!

Quiver and Arrow

Supplies needed:

- (Use 4/20) "Wooden Round Dowels
- (In the colors you would like the Cupid Arrows to be) Spray Paint
- Twine, Lace, Jute, or braided rope (whatever dowels you like to wrap with)
- One Cylinder Jar for your quiver. (I bought mine from Walmart)
- To adorn the bottle, Packaging Sheet or Print Paper
- Scrapbook Paper. (I used glossy cardstock) in the colors that you want the arrows and wings to be. You should use a matching scrap of paper.

Instructions:

1. Brush the dowels with color.
2. To achieve the perfect look, hot glue the ribbon on the dowel (I twisted mine and hot fused both ends).
3. Cut out the arrow and feather
4. Apply hot glue to the arrows and feathers

Directions for Quiver:

1. Cut the paper to the width and length of the cylinder (scrapbook or wrapping)
2. Fasten the document to the cylinder
3. To hold the Cupid Arrows in place, insert the corresponding paper shred inside to
4. If you'd like to, add a matching brace.
5. Now you can put the Cupid Wings anywhere you can, it will look amazing on a door or wall, and your buddies will ask you to make them more! These are beloved by both my kiddos and they both have a collection in their bed.

St. Patrick's Day Shirt

Supplies needed:

- Cricut maker Machine to cut
- Cricut Space Development account
- Cut design with shamrock and doodles
- Infusible Pen Ink 0.04-Green
- Cricut Space Access Design
- Infusible Cricut Tin Jacket
- Easy Press 2 Print
- Card Warehouse
- Butcher Text
- Paper on Laser Printer
- A pre-arranged canvas from Cricut Room to help you get started with this St. Patrick's Day Top!

Instructions:

1. Activate and size the Design Space Cut File to fit your shirt.
2. Send out to cut (draw) the project. Don't forget to have an image mirror. Place the paper with Laser Printer on a standard grip cutting mat. Keep sure to follow the Infusible Ink Pen prompts.
3. Delete the laser printer paper from the cutting mat once the image has been drawn.
4. Place a cardstock sheet inside the shirt where you want your design to be. Place on the shirt and the laser printer paper with the design image side down.Place butcher paper to the laser printer. Following Cricut's recommended heat setting, press the image onto the shirt with the Easy Press.
5. Remove from the shirt the butcher paper, laser printer paper, and card stock and be St. Paddy's Day pinch-proof.

If we're acquainted with the cutting Cricut device family, you're likely familiar with all of the various projects done by you with these instruments, too. The electronic cutting machine or Cricut Joy appears to fit well with a large variety of types of material that the cutting tool can cut.

Coasters Using Infusible Ink for Christmas

Supplies needed:

- Maker Cricut or Explore
- Infusible Ink rounds from Ceramic Coasters
- Buffalo Plaid (Infusible Ink Transmission Sheets)
- Easy Press
- Mat from Easy Press
- Butcher paper
- Cardstock White

Instructions:

1. The prototypes accessible in Design Space with the terms "Everything is good" and "All is Light" were photos
2. On the tile coasters, the Infusible Ink appears so shiny and glossy. I think they'd be great in your house as holiday decor or attach them to a gift package of mugs and hot chocolate.
3. Open the Space File for Christmas Coaster Concept.
4. Print out the patterns from the move sheets of Infusible Paint. Don't hesitate to get th concept replicated.
5. Weed the layouts.
6. Click, in the Heat Guide, to obey the instructions. With a sheet of cardstock underneath the coasters and a strip of butcher paper and over the edge of the Infusible Paint, push for 220 seconds at 390 degrees.
7. Once the coaster has settled, gently cut the transfer cover.

Clear Personalized Labels

Supplies Needed:

- Cricut clear sticker paper
- High-gloss printer paper for the Inkjet printer
- Inkjet printer (check the ink cartridges
- Spatula tool

Instructions:

1. Create a new project in Design Space.
2. Choose the heart shape from the left-hand side Shapes menu.
3. Select an image from the Images menu on the left-hand side menu.
4. Choose a picture of a flower or search for "M55E."
5. Unlock the flower image, position it in the top-left corner of the heart. Make sure it fits without any overhang.
6. Select the heart and the flower, then click on Weld from the bottom-right-hand menu. This ensures that the label is printed together as a unit and not in layers.
7. Select the heart and flowers once again. Then click on Flatten to ensure that only the outline shape of the heart is cut out.
8. Choose "Text" from the left-hand menu. Choose a font, and type the text for your label. You can choose a color for your text.
9. Unlock and move the text into position in the middle of the label.
10. Adjust the size to fit comfortably.
11. Select the heart shape and the font. Then click on Flatten to ensure the label is cut as a whole and not layered.
12. In order not to waste sticker paper, you will want to print as many labels per sheet as you can.
13. Choose the square shape from the *Shapes* menu.
14. Position it on the screen, unlock the shape, and set the measurements to a width of 6 and a height of 9.

15. Move the first label into place at the top-left-hand corner of the screen.
16. Select the label and Duplicate it.
17. Move the second label next to the first one. Give the labels a bit of room between each other and the edges.
18. Fit as many as you can on the sheet, then save your work.
19. Fill in each of the labels with the text you want.
20. If you have space left over when your labels are positioned, you can create smaller ones.
21. You can actually create all different sizes of labels, patterns, and designs.
22. Make sure that all the labels are for print and are flattened.
23. Delete the background recmat.
24. Select all the labels, and click *Attach* from the bottom-right-hand menu.
25. Click Make it, and check that the design and wording are correct before clicking Continue.
26. Choose the high-gloss paper option, and set it to the best quality.
27. Load the sticker paper into the Inkjet printer, and press Send to printer.
28. Choose Sticker paper for the Cricut materials.
29. Load the Stickers into the Cricut, and press Go when it is ready to cut.
30. The Cricut will cut out the stickers, so you can peel them off the backing sheet as and when you need them.

Wedding Invitations

Supplies Needed:

- "Cricut" cutting machine
- Cutting mat
- Cardstock
- Decorative paper/crepe paper/fabric, home printer (if not using "Cricut Maker").

Instructions:

1. Use your "Cricut ID" to log in to the "Design Space" application. Then click on the "New Project" button on the top right corner of the screen to start a new project and view a blank canvas.

2. A beginner-friendly way to create wedding invitations is a customization of an already existing project from the "Design Space" library that aligns with your own ideas. Click on the "Projects" icon on the "Design Panel," then select "Cards" from the "All Categories" drop-down.

3. You can click on the project to preview its description and requirements. Once you have found the project, you want to use, click "Customize" at the bottom of the screen so you can edit the invite and add the required text to it.

4. The design will be loaded onto the canvas. Click on the "Text" button and type in the details for your invite. You will be able to modify the font, color as well as alignment of the text from the "Edit Text Bar" on top of the screen. You can even adjust the size of the entire design as needed. (An invitation card can be anywhere from 6 to 9 inches wide)

5. Select the entire design and click on the "Group" icon on the top right of the screen under "Layers Panel." Then click on the "Save" button to enter a name for your project and click "Save" again.

6. Your design can now be printed then cut. Simply click on the "Make It" button on the top right corner of the screen to view

the required mats and material. Then use your home printer to print the design on your chosen material (white cardstock or paper), or if using the "Cricut Maker," then just follow the prompts on the "Design Space" application.

7. Load the material with printed design to your "Cricut" cutting machine and click "Continue" at the bottom right corner of the screen to start cutting your design.

8. Once your "Cricut" device has been connected to your computer, set the cut setting to "cardstock." Then place the printed cardstock on top of the cutting mat and load it into the "Cricut" device by pushing against the rollers. The "Load/Unload" button would already be flashing, so just press that button first, followed by the flashing "Go" button. Voila! You have your wedding invitations all ready to be put in an envelope and on their way to all your wedding guests.

Custom Notebooks

Supplies Needed:

- "Cricut" cutting machine
- Cutting mat
- Washi sheets
- Decorative paper/crepe paper/fabric

Instructions:

1. Use your "Cricut ID" to log in to the "Design Space" application. Then click on the "New Project" button on the top right corner of the screen to start a new project and view a blank canvas.
2. Let's use an already existing project from the "Cricut" library for this. Click on the "Projects" icon on the "Design Panel" and type in "notebook" in the search bar.
3. You can view all the projects available by clicking on them, and a pop-up window displaying all the details of the project will appear on your screen.
4. Select the project that you like and click on "Customize" so you can further edit this project to your preference.
5. The selected project will be displayed on the Canvas. You can check from the "Layers Panel" if your design contains only one layer, which is very easy to modify, or multiple layers that can be selectively modified. Click on the "Linetype Swatch" to view the color palette and select the desired color for your design.
6. Once you have modified the design to your satisfaction, it is ready to be cut. Simply click on the "Make It" button on the top right corner of the screen to view the required mats and material for your project.
7. Load the washi paper sheet to your "Cricut" cutting machine and click "Continue" at the bottom right corner of the screen to start cutting your design.

8. Connect your "Cricut" device to your computer and place the washi paper or your chosen paper on top of the cutting mat, and load it into the "Cricut" machine by pushing against the rollers. The "Load/Unload" button would already be flashing, so just press that button first, followed by the flashing "Go" button. Voila! Your kids can now enjoy their uniquely customized notebook.

Planner Stickers

Supplies Needed:

- Cricut printable sticker paper
- Cricut Maker
- Cricut standard cutting mat grip
- Printer with ink

Instructions:

1. Choose the sticker designs. You can choose from the Design shop or upload your own.
2. Start by opening the Design Space program and click on the Image option. Then, head to the search function and locate the planner stickers. Locate which one you want to use.
3. Place the choices on the canvas and arrange them in the order that you would like them to be.
4. Click the Make It option. Design Space will direct you to begin printing the image. Follow the directions to print the images.
5. To proceed, place the stickers in the Cricut to cut the stickers out.

Woodland Fox Bookmark

Supplies Needed:

- Cricut weeding tool
- Multiple colors of cardstock
- Adhesive
- Standard cutting mat grip
- Cricut machine

Instructions:

1. Open your Design shop, and use the design file that you have created for this bookmark.
2. You may have to purchase the file that is needed to design this bookmark.
3. Cut two pieces for the bookmark, one for each side of the bookmark. This helps it to be sturdier.
4. You will need to glue the two identical pieces together.
5. Once you send the image to the Cricut machine, you can begin to place the color for your paper on the mat. Then, cut it out. Continue to do this until all the pieces and colors have been cut.
6. Weed out any unnecessary pieces that come out with the fox.
7. Glue the fox together, and then glue it to the bookmark backing. You do not want to use too much glue. This will keep the cardstock from being soggy.
8. Use a heavy book and place the bookmark in between the pages to get the glue to set and the bookmark to not wave.

Coffee Sleeves
Supplies Needed:
- Felt (I used the Cricut felt sheets)
- Iron-on Vinyl (I used the sparkle vinyl in silver)
- Cricut Cutting Machine
- Weeding instruments (optional)
- Cricut Easy-Press (optional)
- Velcro
- Texture paste or sewing machine
- Cut file

Instructions:
1. Start by cutting your pieces. Cut the words from sparkle iron-on vinyl using your fine point cutting edge. Make sure to reflect the cuts on the iron-on vinyl and spot its glossy side down on your mat. Cut the sleeve itself from felt. On the off chance that you need to mark your cutting in both of the sleeves one after another, you might need to change the settings inside Design Space to make the most of your material. It needs to cut every sleeve from one sheet of felt.
2. Start by featuring your first mat with a sleeve. At that point, click on the sleeve itself.
3. Next, select the second mat that has a sleeve. Click the sleeve itself and then the three dots. At that point, pick "move to another mat."
4. Pick the mat with the principal sleeve.
5. You simply need to turn it and move the position so it isn't covering the first. You would now be able to cut two sleeves from one sheet of felt.
6. Remove all material excess from your vinyl pattern, including the focuses of your letters.
7. Now stick your letters and velcro to the sleeves to finish them.

Earrings for Women

Supplies Needed:

- Faux leather
- Cricut machine (any of them will work the faux leather)
- Jewelry accessories (jump rings)
- Jewelry pliers (two sets are needed when working with jump rings)
- Leather punch for gaps
- Cut file

Instructions:

1. Start by downloading a free SVG record and transferring it to your Cricut machine. If you are having issues with the process, look back at previous instructions. Then resize the document accordingly before cutting. To cut the faux leather, place the material face down on the mat.

2. At that point, place your cuts in Cricut Design Space and pick fake leather as your material. Cut the faux leather with your machine.

3. When the cut is finished, remove the mat from the machine and strip back the extra material to uncover your cut hoops.

4. Then remove the studs themselves from the mat. Remember that pieces cut from the internal parts of the studs may make adorable hoops themselves, so don't dispose of anything until you have used the entirety of the pieces you need.

5. To gather the hoops, use your weeding instrument to puncture the highest point of every single one.

6. At that point, use your jewelry pliers to open up the circle in the opening or to expand the bounce ring contingent upon how you are making your hoop.

Pet Name Collars

Supplies Needed:

- Heat transfer vinyl
- Cricut EasyPress (or iron)
- Green StandardGrip mat
- Cricut Fine-Point Blade
- Weeding tool
- Scraper tool

Instructions:

1. Start a new project in Design Space.
2. Measure the color to get the length and width.
3. Choose "Square" from the "Shapes" menu on the left-hand side menu.
4. Set the square's color to grey.
5. Unlock the shape and set the dimensions accordingly.
6. Choose a picture of either a dog or a cat (depending on the pet).
7. Choose a collar and size it to be able to fit onto the shape.
8. You will want to use the image a few times across the collar.
9. Use image #M10402B. It is a black cat hissing.
10. Size it down and make 5 copies of it.
11. Select the fifth cat and flip it horizontally so it is facing the other cat images.
12. Make 3 copies of the flipped cat picture.
13. Select the "Heart" shape from the "Shapes" menu from the left-hand side menu.
14. Unlock it and size it to the same scale as the cat to fit onto the collar.
15. Change the heart color to red.
16. Make 6 duplicates of the heart.
17. Select 'Text," choose a font, make the color red, and type in the pet's name.
18. Position the name in the center of the collar (the square).

19. Place the cat facing left at one end and a cat facing right at the opposite end of the collar.
20. Place a heart next to the cat on either end of the collar.
21. Place another cat after the heart, then another heart, etc.
22. Make this pattern for both sides of the collar ending by the name.
23. Select and remove the grey square.
24. Hold down the "Ctrl" key on the keyboard and select each of the cats.
25. Right-click and select attach.
26. Do the same for the hearts and include the name in the selection.
27. Click "Make it."
28. The cutting screen will show two cutting mats, each with a different color.
29. You will notice that the cats and the hearts with the writing are correctly spaced as you laid them out.
30. Choose "Mirror" as it is heat transfer, so it needs to be mirrored to iron the image onto the collar.
31. Cut the corresponding vinyl color a few inches larger than the grey square was.
32. Stick the cut vinyl to the green cutting mat and load it into the Cricut machine.
33. Make sure the fine-point blade is loaded.
34. Click "Continue," choose the correct material, and ensure the dial is on custom.
35. Click "Go" when the Cricut is ready to cut.
36. Once it has finished cutting, remove the design from the Cricut.
37. Stick the next color vinyl sheet (cut to the correct size) onto the green cutting mat.
38. Load it into the Cricut.
39. Check that all the settings and materials are correct.
40. Do not forget to "Mirror" the image.
41. When the Cricut is ready to cut, press "Go."

42. When the cutting is done, use the weeding tool to clean up the designs.
43. Start off with the cat transfer design.
44. Place it facedown on the collar.
45. Place a cloth over the transfer paper.
46. Use a pre-heated Cricut EasyPress or iron to push down, heating the vinyl onto the collar.
47. After 30 seconds, use the brayer tool or scraping tool to go over the design.
48. When the transfer has cooled down, peel the backing paper off.
49. When you are done, you will have a personalized pet collar that any animal lover would love as a gift.

PART 2.

CRICUT MACHINE AND ACCESSORIES

Chapter 1.
What Is the Cricut Explore Air 2

Cricut Explore Air 2

This is the youngest sibling of the Cricut Explore line. It is the best of the machines in this line. Explore Air 2 is as efficient as the other ones, but it does its work even better. It even has a better design, and it comes in different colors than you can choose. The Cricut Explore Air 2 is the current top-selling craft plotter from Cricut and is probably the best value they can give for the price. This model cuts materials at twice the speed of both the previous ones and has Bluetooth support and two adapter clamps on board. The storage cup at the top of the unit features a smaller shallower cut to hold your replacement blade while they aren't in use. If you want to swap to a different project between several different tips, they're all readily accessible. All cups have a smooth silicone rim, so you won't have to worry about your blades getting rusty or scratched.

It is the perfect tool for the job for someone who finds themselves using their Cricut with some frequency. You will be able to do your crafts twice as quickly, and each time, even at that pace, you will get a favorable outcome!

Capability

The model features a Fast mode that speeds up the cutting process, primarily if you work with deadlines. It also has the features in the other systems like the German carbide premium blade, inbuilt Bluetooth adapter, dual carriage, and auto-settings. The great thing about Explore Air is that it is ideal for both beginners and advanced users.

Materials

This machine can cut through a hundred materials or even more. This includes and is not limited to cotton, silk, tissue paper, corkboard, foil, foam, aluminum, leather, clay, chipboard, burlap, and even birch wood.

It also has the Smart Dial, which helps you manage the cutting width depending on the materials.

Cutting Force

The model is highly potent, and it makes use of the German carbide premium fine point blade, which comes with precision and speed. It is also able to cut any material with a width of 11.5 x 23.5 inches. When you first purchase a Cricut Explore Air 2, you get a three months free subscription with access to premium features offered by Cricut!

The Cricut Design Space is also cloud-based for those using iOS devices. With this, you can work offline! The only downside in this model is the slightly increased noise level, but this is expected because it works two times faster than the previous models.

Your shiny, new Cricut Explore Air 2 will look like this:

- Cricut Explore Air 2 machine.

- Adapter.

- Power and USB cord.

- German carbide premium blade.

- Machine software and application.

- Built-in projects and images.

- Standard Grip cutting mat.

- Cardstock Sample.

- A pen.

- Welcome guide.

How to Get Started

The Explore Air 2 is compatible with Smart devices such as Tablets, Smartphones, and Pcs. This is a very helpful feature. For example, you can create a design while in transit and click print when you get home.

Now you just purchased the Cricut Explore Air 2 machine, confused on how to set it up?

Follow these easy steps to set up your Explore Air 2;

For IOS/ android

- After you must have plugged your machine, switch it on, pair your device with the Cricut machine via Bluetooth.

- Download and install Design space.

- Launch the app, sign in or create a Cricut ID.

- Tap Menu and select "machine setup" and "App overview."

- Choose a new machine set up.

- Follow on-screen directions to complete the setup.

-

To set up this Cricut Explore Machine, here are some of the steps to follow:

- Plug the machine in and turn it on.

- Enter your browser, go to DesignCricut.Com/Setup.

- Follow the directions on the screen to sign-up or create your Cricut ID and press submit.

- Download and install the design or software. You will be asked to do your first project with that you will know that your setup is complete.

- You will need to set up your machine with your personal computer and perform your first project on the Cricut.

It is recommended to know the exact spot to place your machine before proceeding to set up the machine. It is more recommended to put your machine near your computer or where you will be using another connected device such as a tablet.

Even though the Cricut cutter can operate wirelessly without connecting directly to a computer, it is ideal for you to be near the machine for easy access to load and unload mats as well as pressing the necessary buttons.

You should also consider which perfect surface to place the machine on—a flat surface 10 inches from the machine will be a great choice to guide against unloaded mats falling on the floor or hanging awkwardly.

You will need a range of 10 inches of space above the top of your machine. This space creates a room to open the lid of the machine and easily put things like the pen into the Cricut machine.

The following steps will show you how to set up your machine correctly:

- Plugin your machine to the power source with the power adaptor and switch it on.

- Connect your Cricut explore machine to the computer using the USB cable.

- Open the web browser on your computer and log on to the Cricut website. Login if you already have a Cricut account, but if you are new, go-ahead to set up a Cricut account on the website.

- After creating your account, you are now ready to set up your Cricut machine by connecting to the design portal on the Cricut website.

- Click on the download icon to download the latest plugin software.

- After implementing the above process, the below steps will guide you through the completion of the installation process, either you are a Mac or a PC user.

Installation Setup for Mac

- After downloading the software, click and open the Finder in the Mac toolbar.

- The next step is to locate the downloaded folder on your computer and double-click the Cricut Design Space file you already downloaded.

- The terms and conditions will come up, review, and agree to it.

- Drag to the right the np—Cricut plugin into the Internet Plugin folder.

- After this, click the authenticate icon.

- After you have authenticated the Internet Plugins, close the Cricut Design Space and download the windows frame to return to your Mac browser.

- Get out of your browser and return to the Cricut website to continue with the setup process.

- Click on the "Detect Machine" icon and click continue when your Cricut machine has been detected.

- If you do not want to subscribe to the software, check the box to enable your trial subscription and tap the continue button.

- After this, you will receive a thank you note denoting that your Cricut Explore Air 2 is all set up for your first cutting project.

- As a hint to take full advantage of the free trial subscription, do make sure you check the open trial box before you click continue. This page comes up for both the Mac and PC installation process.

- Also, your free trial subscriptions allow you to access the Cricut image library of over 30,000 images and 300 fonts without a credit card or any other requirements needed.

Installation for PC

- After downloading the Plugin software to your PC, close your browser.

- Tap the start menu and click to open the documents folder.

- Select downloads and double-click the Cricut Design Space file to open the setup of the file.

- Then click continue when the setup is on.

- Review the terms and conditions and click the accept button.

- Follow the directions to install the software.

- When you have successfully installed the Cricut Design Space software, click the finish button.

- Next, tap on the "Detect Machine" icon. When your machine has been detected, tap "continue."

- Check the box to access the free trial subscription, and then click continue.

- You will also get the thank you card to ascertain that your Cricut Machine is set up and that you are ready to carry out your first cut.

Pairing the Cricut Machine Through Bluetooth to the Computer

To get your Cricut Explore Air 2 paired with your computer or mobile device, you are required to take the following steps:

- Make sure your Wireless Bluetooth Adapter is in place and working.

- Have the Cricut Explore Air 2 turned on, and it should be at most 15 feet from your PC.

- Check to be sure your computer is Bluetooth enabled by taking the following sub-steps on your computer.

- Go to the "Start button" and right-click on it.

- Select the "Device Manager."

- If you have the Bluetooth listed in the device manager, it is definitely Bluetooth enabled; otherwise, you will have to get a USB device referred to as Bluetooth Dongle to get your computer interacting with the other Bluetooth devices.

- You can now close your Device manager once you have confirmed it is Bluetooth enabled.

- Go to the "Start menu."

- Select "Settings."

- Go to the "Devices" option and open it.

- Make sure the Bluetooth is active and select "Include Bluetooth or another device."

- Click on "Bluetooth," you can then grab a cup of coffee while your PC searches for and pairs with the Cricut Machine.

- Select the Cricut machine once it appears on the list.

- In a case where you are prompted to input in a PIN, type in 0000 and click on "Connect."

- The Cricut Explore Air 2 machine might show up as an Audio on the Bluetooth list. If this happens, it is okay, and you can go ahead with pairing.

- In a situation where you have multiple Cricut machines, make use of the device code in identifying which one you like to pair. The device code can be found on the serial number tag at the bottom of the machine.

Chapter 2.
The Indispensable Tools

Tools and Accessories Needed to Work With Explore Air 2 Machine

Thanks to Cricut machines and all the blades you can use with different models, you are set to find out how crafting can be more rewarding, simpler, and easier with additional tools and accessories. Aside from blades and tips created and designed for different purposes, fabrics, crafting materials, some Cricut tools, and accessories can make your crafting and DIY projects more successful and rewarding.

Weeding Tools

Some crafting projects just call for the use of weeders, a.k.a. weeding tools. There are several different Cricut weeding tools, each handy in its way, and proposed for different weeding techniques.

Weeding tools are particularly handy if you are working with iron-on and vinyl, and you need to remove excessive material as you are working on your project. Weeding tools can also be very helpful for removing excess glitter and glue.

Regular weeding tools available as a part of the Cricut toolset will do a great job of removing excess material and adhesives from your projects. Another option is going for the hooked weeding tool that looks much like something you would find in a dentistry toolkit. Many crafters find this tool to be efficient and precise

Tweezers

What crafter wouldn't make good use out of a quality pair of tweezers? There are four different types of Cricut tweezers, each designed with a different angle, so crafters may choose the most suitable tool for their project's needs. If your projects require regular work with small parts and most of the work is "touchy," you will like the idea of owning a pair of fine tweezers. Reverse tweezers may seem a bit strange to a crafter used to working with regular or fine tweezers as these tweezers work in a reverse way. When you apply the pressure and squeeze the reverse tweezers, it opens instead of closing.

Cricut Scissors

Cutting but with no scissors in your toolkit? Your Cricut machine can do most of the cutting, but a crafter still needs their scissors, right? So, you don't need to buy Cricut scissors – if you have a pair of scissors that work great for you, there is no need for changing your tools. In case you decided to look for a pair of quality scissors, Cricut models may be suitable for your needs. Basic scissors have a rather small cutting part and might not be particularly comfortable to use. The second model, fabric scissors, has a 5-inch blade that is designed to cut through thick materials

Brayer

Every crafter uses adhesives, which makes brayer a rather handy piece of tool to add to your Cricut station. Cricut brayer has an ergonomic design, which means that it is pretty easy and simple to use while also very comfortable. You are set to love using brayer as you can easily avoid wrinkles and bubbles when applying adhesives to your fabric. The brayer is perfect for thick materials, while you can also use it for stamping and making prints. The brayer performs intended operations smoothly, including adhering fabric to your mat in case you are using mat Fabric Grip for your projects.

Scoring Tool

If you are planning to buy Cricut Maker or you already own this model, you won't need the Cricut scoring tool as Cricut Maker has a Quick Swap Scoring Wheel tip that can help you make folds and 3D projects. In case you are using one of the other available Cricut machine models and need a tool to help you with folding and scoring, you will love the scoring tool by Cricut. You can use the scoring tool manually for making folds or insert it into the Cricut Explore tool cartridge.

Cricut Trimmer

As a part of the Essential tool kit by Cricut, you will get a trimmer that can help you cut different types of materials quickly and without much effort. Regardless of what type of projects you are working on, having a quality trimmer is helpful.

Cricut Spatula

In case you take your regular use of paper in crafting projects seriously, you will mark the use of spatula as necessary and even mandatory.

The size of the Cricut spatula is suitable for larger pieces of material, while you can also work with smaller pieces of paper. To avoid tearing the paper pieces when removing the paper from the Cricut machine, you can easily slip the spatula between the mat and paper pieces. Once you start using a spatula, make sure to clean it often.

Cricut Mats

Every type of Cricut crafting material has recommended Cricut mats depending on which projects you are working on and what materials you are cutting. You can find recommended mats for your projects and make the best out of every cut you make with your machine. Mats aim to support your materials and fabrics.

Therefore, it is important to choose your mats to match your preferred materials and specifications of the crafting project you are working on. It is important to learn which type of mat fits the requirements of your projects as Design Space won't suggest which mat to use for a specific project.

Accessories

The accessories and tools often do overlap in some ways since a lot of these tools are accessories, such as the perforation tool and scraping tools. However, there is more available than just that, and below, you'll learn of the important accessories that can help you make the most of your machine.

- **Deep cut blade:** This helps you cut wood and leather, and you can buy these individually.

- **Bonded fabric blade:** This can cut through fabric that's been bonded with stabilizers such as Heat N Bond.

- **Cutting Mats:** These will be used for crafting pretty much anything, and if you're using lighter materials or heavier lines, you should get both a LightGrip and a strong grip cutting mat. These are useful for a variety of projects.

- **Toolsets:** We discussed tools in the previous section, but they are essential to help you with your Cricut projects.

- **Scoring Stylus:** While the Maker model has this included, picking up scoring stylus accessories for other models can help you make anything requiring precise folding. These can help you fold pretty much any project by giving you neat score lines, taking out all the guesswork!

- **Pens:** These are useful not just for scoring and cutting but also writing—you can address letters and cards directly from your Cricut machine. There is no more signing a bunch of cards!

- **Aluminum Foil Ball:** Hey, look—a Cricut accessory that isn't something you need to go to a craft store or Amazon for! This will keep your blades clean and sharp, so you don't need to spend extra money buying replacements. Plus, you don't have to travel far to find it, you may even have some in your kitchen!

- **Fabric Marking Pen:** If you plan on using your Cricut machine for cutting fabric, this is something that you should consider buying. It will save you a bunch of time.

These accessories are items that you either already have or items that you may not have even thought about. But purchasing a few of these will certainly help you use your Cricut machine, that's for sure.

Chapter 3.
What Can Be Done to Sell and How to Do It

With this device, you can do something and produce countless Cricut suggestions. The basic rule here is to let your imagination know no limits. If you produce a scrapbook, the primary objective is creating designs, which will live with the photographs that you invest.

Let us say, for instance, you place in photos of your wedding. You must choose or create a style, which would create an environment that can make anybody who looks at the scrapbooks and the pictures relive the memories. The same basic rule is going to apply to anyone. You can likewise produce income because of this by assisting individuals in thinking of designs for their scrapbooks.

The utilization of the software program is not restricted to just producing scrapbooks. As stated before, it also allows your creativity to set the boundaries, and with its use, there ought to be no limits.

Probably the most typical development originating from a Cricut printer, apart from scrapbooks, is the Cricut calendars. You can utilize the designs that you receive from a Cricut machine to add spice and life to any calendar.

With all the use of a Cricut computer and the application tools, you can make layouts for every month of a calendar year. The key here is selecting some design, which can focus on what that month is about. Take October as a good example, wherein the very best design is surely a background depicting October fest. Therefore, there you have it, some fantastic Cricut ideas that will help you generate income or simply allow you to be happy. Cricut tasks are something that you can do with your Cricut cutting machine. It can easily be something out of easy tasks, which could provide you with private pleasure to help you get revenue. In past times, people regard this printer as only a scrapbooker's tool. However, with the increasing ingenuity of humanity, suggestions are growing like crazy.

Individuals had to learn that the Cricut cutting printer is only a die-cutting device. That is, it is not a person that is directly accountable for the development of the designs. You can find designs via software tools and cartridges. Almost all that Cricut printers cut the models that the person chooses from the program or cartridges, and nothing more. The application, which is responsible for producing models for the many Cricut tasks, will be the Cricut Design Studio. This has hundreds of designs you can pick from them. You can create your own designs too, and edit those that are in their library already. When you have selected your design, use the Cricut printer to cut it out, and you are all set for prime time.

Greeting cards are but one project that you can utilize the Cricut device for. Many people usually have their own design that they have conceptualized and imprinted onto their minds.

The majority of the time, the mall that you visit will not keep the layout that you are looking for. Occasionally they may, but that is a leap of faith. With the entire Cricut machine, you can create your own design and be satisfied with it.

You can offer the cards that you develop and earn money; today, that is the business male mindset for you! This move can help ease frustration and stress and enable you to attain tranquility or peace. Calendars could be a consideration. Calendars have twelve months in a year, and every one of those months has its own identity. With all the assistance of a Cricut cutting machine, you can help give life to all those weeks. Ensure you develop or chose styles that could help paint the spirits of the month or something that is related to them. Invitations can also be great Cricut jobs. You decide on a style that suits the occasion, and afterward, you have it cut through the Cricut cutting machine. The key is usually to never ever allow your imagination to relax. Ensure you keep it going, and you will have far more projects worked on.

Selling Pre-Cut Customized Vinyl

Vinyl is a beginner-friendly material to work with and comes in a variety of colors and patterns to add to its great reputation. You can create customized labels for glass containers and canisters to help anyone looking to organize their pantry. Explore the online trends and adjust the labels. Once you have your labels designed, the easiest approach is to set up an Etsy shop, which is free and very easy to use. It is almost like opening an Amazon prime membership account. If your design is in demand, you will have people ordering even with no advertising. But if you would like to keep the tempo high, then advertise your Etsy listing on Pinterest and other social media platforms. This is a sure-shot way to generate more traffic to your Etsy shop and to turn potential customers into paying customers. An important note here is the pictures being used on your listing.

You cannot use any of the stock images from the Design Space application, but you must use your own pictures that match the product you are selling.

Create a package of five or six different labels, like sugar, salt, rice, oats, beans, etc., that can be sold as a standard package. Offer a customized package that will allow the customer to request any word that they want to be included in their set. Since these labels weigh next to nothing, shipping can easily be managed with standard mail, with usually only a single postage stamp, depending on the delivery address. Make sure you do not claim the next day or two-day delivery for these. Build enough delivery time so you can create and ship the labels without any stress.

Once you have an established business model, you can adjust the price and shipping of your product (more on that later). Check out other Etsy listings to make sure your product pricing is competitive enough, and you are attracting enough potential buyers.

Now, once you have traction in the market, you can offer additional vinyl-based projects like bumper stickers, iron-on designs, or heat-transfer vinyl designs that people can transfer on their clothing using a standard heating iron. Really, once you have gained some clientele, you can modify and customize all your listings to develop a one-stop-shop for all things vinyl (a great name for your future Etsy shop, right!).

Selling Finished Pieces

You would be using your Cricut machines for a variety of personal projects like home décor, holiday décor, personalized clothing, and more. Next time you embark on another one of your creative journeys leading to unique creations, just make two of everything, and you can easily put the other product to sell on your Etsy shop. Another great advantage is that you will be able to save all your projects on the Design Space application for future use, so if one of your projects goes viral, you can easily buy the supplies and turn them into money-making offerings. This way, not only is your original idea for personal use pay off, but you can make much more money than you invested, to begin with.

Again, spend some time researching what kind of designs and decorations are trending in the market, and use them to spark up inspiration for your next project. Some of the current market trends include customized cake and cupcake toppers and watercolor designs that can be framed as fancy wall decorations. The cake toppers can be made with cardstock, which is another beginner-friendly material, light in weight, and can be economically shipped, tucked inside an envelope.

Design and Sell Personalized Clothing and Accessories

T-shirts with cool designs and phrases are all the rage right now. Just follow a similar approach to the selling vinyl section and take it up a notch. You can create sample clothing with iron-on designs and market it with tag lines like "can be customized further at no extra charge" or "transfer the design on your own clothing" to get traction in the market.

You can buy sling bags and customize them with unique designs to be sold as finished products at a higher price than a plain, boring sling bag.

Consider creating a line of products with a centralized theme like the DC Marvel characters or the Harry Potter movies, and design custom T-shirts, hats, and even bodysuits for babies.

You can create customized party boxes and gift bags at the request of the customer. Once your product has a dedicated customer base, you can get project ideas from them directly and quote them a price for your work. Is not that great?

Another big advantage of the heat-transfer vinyl, as mentioned earlier, is that anyone can transfer the design on their desired item of clothing using a standard household iron.

But you would need to include the transfer directions with the order, letting them know exactly how to prep for the heat-transfer process so as not to damage their clothing item.

Again, heat-transfer vinyl can be easily shipped using a standard mailing envelope.

Design and Sell Stickers

If you have a knack for design, then making unique stickers could be your way to start a side-hustle with your Cricut. Stickers are easy to make, and there are plenty of ideas and themes that you can think of to create unique designs.

Design and Sell Cellphone Cases

From quotes to superheroes, colors to motifs—the sky is your limit in designing unique, one-of-a-kind cellphone cases. You can even start with personalized cases for friends and family.

Design and Sell Nail Decals

If you love doing your nails, then you know there is a market for cute and unique decals for fingernails. This is an option not many have considered, so you could be one of the first people.

Design and Sell Cricut Earrings

If you are okay with spending some time weeding out small cuts from intricate designs, then you might want to consider creating Cricut earrings.

Design and Sell Window Decals

Everyone has a peculiar image, an object we are practically obsessed with. Getting a vinyl window decal of one's favorite image will go a long way in giving your decor a boost. Making and selling window decals is quite easy and profitable.

Make and Sell Canvas Wall Art

Customized wall art would generate quick and easy money. Get inspirational sayings or designs, and make them into wall art for sale.

Design and Sell Onesies

Onesies or bodysuits are generally cute clothes, which can be made better with amazing artwork. Onesies for babies can be made with a lot of text, such as "Daddy loves you" or "Momma's baby." Other mushy word art can be used in designing onesies for kids.

Design and Sell Hoodies

Hoodies are a great wear for cold seasons. A designed one would roll better with the youth. The design can be preordered too.

Design and Sell Leather Neck Piece

A leather pendant can be designed for a necklace and sold out to interested buyers.

Design and Sell Banners

Banners can be made for celebrations, festive periods, camping, parties, religious activities, or sporting activities. All these can be made and sold.

Design and Sell Window Clings

Window clings with the design of the seasons can be made and sold. Other designs or images can also be used for creating window clings.

Design and Sell Stencils

Stencils can be created and sold for those that want to hand-paint a post or sign. It would also generate a nice amount of money.

Design and Sell Safari Animal Stickers

Stickers of safari animals are attractive items. They can be sold to animal-lovers. The sticker is easy to make and will also be a source of income generation.

Design and Sell Customized Decals

Customized stickers are exceptional because they are adaptable to a myriad of uses, from events to home decor. When you offer a custom-designed provider, it is differentiation that the larger stores cannot compete with.

Design and Sell Kids-Related Wall Decals

Youngsters like redecorating all year round. From nurseries to birthday parties to toddler showers, there is no way-finishing want for child and children decor.

Design and Sell Wedding Decor and Favors

The wedding industry is alive and well; that is no wonder. In step with Pinterest, yard weddings are on an upward trend.

The look for them has gone up 441%. Everybody is attempting to store a little at their wedding.

Design and Sell Paper Flowers

Similar to farmhouse decor, the recognition of paper plants is at an all-time high, with more than half a million searches for it on Pinterest each month. They are good for all occasions, from Mother's Day to weddings to baby showers. It is no wonder since they are in such high demand.

Design and Sell Cricut Cake Toppers

Cake and cupcake toppers might be the easiest and cost-effective things to make. Parents are constantly looking to up their game at children's birthday parties with all styles of custom-designed decor.

Unicorns are all the rage these days with kids. I have, in my opinion, made three units of unicorn birthday decor (that are all included in my aid library, by the way). Youngsters are enthusiastic about unicorns.

Design and Sell Leather Earrings

Lovable, leather jewelry takes no graphic design abilities to make. In case you just need to test the waters, move to get a gaggle of unfastened leather swatches from furniture stores and use them to make an initial batch. My templates for those rings are included in my useful resource library.

Design and Sell Felt and Fabric Flowers

Cactus arrangement searches were up 235% in 2019 on Pinterest. Get in the succulent fashion with succulent felt.

Design and Sell Wood Letters

There are extra than a million searches a month on Pinterest for rustic signs and hangings. Coincidentally, you could cut wood with your Cricut Maker! Customized wood signs are a sure guess.

Design and Sell Labeling Stickers

Labeling stickers can be made for labeling things in the house. Things in the kitchen, pantry, playroom, classroom, and other places can be labeled with labeling stickers.

Design and Sell Labeling Vinyl

Labeling adhesive vinyl can be made for labeling things in the house. Things in the kitchen, pantry, playroom, classroom, and other places can be labeled with labeling vinyl.

Design and Cut Appliqués

Fancy fabrics can be made into appliqués to design or decorate a place or object.

Design and Sell Christmas Ornaments

Christmas is a period people celebrate and when people decorate their workplaces, abodes, and religious settings, among others.

Market Research

Etsy

Before you sell on Etsy, I will advise you to set up a website first and then head to sell on Etsy. Etsy is a place where people sell their vintage, handcrafted, custom, or unique products. There are so many people there already selling their craft, and you can also join them to sell yours. Then, take your Etsy and pin it for people on Pinterest as well. The pictures of your work should be outstanding to attract people to buy your product. You know that people buy looks before they buy the actual product.

Vendor Markets

One of the fastest ways to make a good bit of cash is to participate in an outdoor vendor market, especially in the fall or close to the holidays. During this time of year, customers are keeping their eyes peeled for gifts, and there are plenty of festivals and markets to participate in. This is a good way to meet potential customers, gain exposure, and network with other vendors.

There are many things to consider when deciding whether you would like to participate in a market. While it can be quick cash, because your customers are all in one place and expecting to spend money, you must plan well in advance. Before committing to participating, you should consider:

- **Set up:** Is there enough color space for you to display your products pleasingly? Does your space have everything you need to run your booth (electricity, Wi-Fi, etc.)? What will your booth look like?

- **Time commitment:** Are you able to prepare ahead of time? Can you be at the market for the full duration?

- **Security for money:** Never leave your money unattended!

- **Upfront cost:** Most markets require a booth rental fee. You will also need to make products beforehand.

- **Payment:** How will you accept payment? Do you have the means for electronic payment methods such as Square, PayPal, etc.?

- **Assistants:** Is there anyone who can help you set up, man the booth, and pack up?

Not all markets are created equal. Some draw in large crowds, and others have very few customers. To find out which ones are best for you, I recommend talking to other vendors who have participated. This will help you decide if a market is worth the time, money, and effort that it takes to participate.

If you decide to set up a booth at a market, be sure to have ways to communicate with your customers. Have plenty of business cards on hand, and include your social media accounts and email. You may want to consider passing out free samples such as small decals made from scrap vinyl or holding a raffle to draw customers to your booth. Be sure to interact with your customers by greeting them and offering assistance. Nothing makes a customer want to walk away faster than a vendor who shows no interest in the customer.

Social Media

Through platforms such as Instagram, Facebook, Pinterest, and YouTube, you can share your products, connect with customers all around the world, and learn from other business owners. It is free, easy, and powerful. The more likes, comments, and followers you have, the more people will see your posts. These applications also offer paid ads to promote your business and reach more users. Once your business account is set up, you can post photos and videos, send and receive messages, and receive notifications for comments and likes. They also offer analytical data that show you how many people saw your posts, along with other information. All of this is accessible from your computer or smartphone. You can make any of the craft you find easy and post pictures of it online, announcing to those on your list that it is for sale. This works better because whoever is buying gets to see the picture of whatever he is getting before ordering it. Personalized crafts should also be included in your order of business. Facebook is probably the one that most of us are familiar with, as it has been around longer than the others. In addition to setting up a business page to promote your items, you can also create a group. If you manage a group, you decide who is in it, and you can make posts that only those people can see. It offers a layer of privacy if you prefer that, but it also allows you to target your posts to your audience. Instagram is another popular application. Followers and hashtags are important to having your posts visible to more people. It can be linked to your Facebook account so that you can post your Instagram posts directly onto Facebook without having to recreate them in the Facebook application. The more hashtags, likes, and followers your posts have, the more people will see them.

Pinterest and YouTube can be useful applications as well, although I have never received a sale that was driven by either of them. I believe these platforms would be useful for reaching customers who are looking for how-to videos and ideas, which may be a direction you would like to take your business. Many people make money from YouTube channels once advertisers are willing to advertise on their channels.

We are all aware of how social media has become a marketing platform for not only established corporations but also small businesses and budding entrepreneurs. Simply add hashtags for sale, product, selling, free shipping, a sample included, and more to entice potential buyers. Join Facebook Community pages and groups for handcraft sellers and buyers to market your products. Use catchy phrases like "customization available at no extra cost" or "free returns if not satisfied" when posting the products on these pages as well as your personal Facebook page. Use Twitter to share feedback from your satisfied customers to widen your customer base. You can do this by creating a satisfaction survey that you can email to your buyers or include a link to your Etsy listing, asking for online reviews and ratings from your customers.

Another tip here is to post pictures of anything and everything you have created using Cricut machines, even those that you did not plan to sell. You never know who else might need something that you deemed unsellable. Since you will be creating these only after the order has been placed, you can easily gather the required supplies after the fact and get crafting.

Target Local Farmer's Markets and Boutiques

If you like the thrill of a show-and-tell, then reserve a booth at a local farmer's market, and show up with some ready-to-sell crafts. In this case, you are relying on the number of people attending and a subset of those who might be interested in purchasing from you. If you are in an urban neighborhood where people are keenly interested in unique art designs but do not have the time to create them on their own, you can easily make big bucks by setting a decent price point for your products.

Bring flyers to hand out to people, so they can reach you through one of your social media accounts or email and check all your existing Etsy listings. Think of these events as a means of marketing for those who are not as active online but can be excited with customized products to meet their next big life event like a baby shower, birthday party, or wedding. One downside to participating in local events is the generation of mass inventory and booth displays, topped with expenses to load and transport the inventory. You may or may not be able to sell all of the inventory, depending on the size of the event, but as I said earlier, you can still make the most of this by marketing your products and building up a local clientele.

Online Selling Platforms

The most well-known online selling platform for handmade items is probably Etsy, but there are others such as Amazon Handmade. Before setting up your online shop, you can read the site's handbook and determine if the fees are worth it to you. Online shops require a good knowledge of SEO so that your items can be found among the competition—and there is a lot of competition! These shops are easy to run since the website is provided for you, and customers are already drawn to the site. Your shop will not run itself, though, and it takes a good bit of time and effort on the shop owner's part. Photos, descriptions, and SEO require a good bit of time and effort.

Wholesale and Consignment

Quite often, vinyl craft business owners have the option to sell their products through wholesale or consignment. Through a wholesale arrangement, you sell your product at a lower price to another business owner (usually a store owner), who will then sell the product at a retail price and keep the profit. This is a little different from consignment. In a consignment situation, you stock your products in a storefront and price the items how you wish. When your items sell, the store owner keeps a percentage (usually 20% or 30%), and you receive the rest of the money from the sale.

There are pros and cons to wholesale and consignment. The obvious benefit from these arrangements is that your items can be featured and displayed in a store that potentially brings in customers, which can lead to more sales. Customers are also likely to hear about your business and buy from you in the future if they like to support local businesses. One of the downfalls to consignment and wholesale is deciding if the work is worth the money you receive in return. You will need to decide the cost to sell your items at wholesale or price them at consignment for you to make a reasonable profit that is worth your time and work. It is also possible that the store draws in few customers, and your stocked products do not sell. If you agree to sell your items on wholesale or consignment, be sure to have a written agreement between yourself and the shop owner to avoid future problems.

No matter how you decide to market your products, be sure to follow copyright and trademark laws, and file your taxes.

All of these marketing methods are full of competition, so finding your niche—what makes you stand out—is the name of the game. Market research can help define what your target audience is looking for, which can lead you to develop your products around the people who buy from you. For example, my most common customers are females who are looking for unique shirts and gifts, so I try to stay on top of what is trending in these categories. I then showcase my products on social media, which generates customers. I have found that while my customers could order custom shirts and gifts online, they prefer the flexibility and customer service that I offer.

eBay

You could upload your craft to eBay and sell them there.

Become a Cricut Affiliate

This entails being paid to make tutorial videos by Cricut, the company. These videos are uploaded to the internet for the netizens to make use of them. To become a Cricut affiliate, you need to have a strong internet presence. You must also have a tangible number of followers on your social media accounts.

Post Tutorial Videos on Your Vlog

This has nothing to do with being an affiliate; rather, you create a blog for videos, upload tutorial videos, and get paid through the traffic generated.

Facebook Groups

This is another nice place you could sell your designs in. A lot of people make sales daily on Facebook, and you can join them too. If your designs are beautiful and you take good pictures of the designs and post them on a Facebook group, you will have a lot of people placing an order for them.

If people are ready to buy across your locality, you should be prepared to ship it to them. For the group to not see your post as spam, you need to join groups that are into handmade designs or crafts. There are many of them out there that you can search and join today.

Craft Fairs

You can set up at a craft fair to make it tons of stuff. Go to a craft fair in your locality, where you find a lot of handmade products there to sell. When you go to such a place, you can also sell your craft there.

Making Money Through Teaching

There are so many of your friends that may have gotten a Cricut machine yet do not know how to use it. Many may have gotten it but still, need to be taught how to use the machine effectively. This is where you have to come in and teach them how to use the machine and how to do special designs. Teaching how to make designs with Cricut is not limited to face-to-face contact only. You can open a YouTube channel and teach a lot of people about how to make designs. The good thing with a YouTube channel is that people will tell you what you should be teaching them. Many will suggest the next video you should be making.

As you teach them on YouTube, you may not make money directly from them except if some decide to send you some tips. However, you can still make money from them through affiliate marketing. Many of them will watch your channel but do not have Cricut yet and would like to buy one. If they use your affiliate link, you will earn some commission through the purchase. The beauty of affiliate marketing with Amazon is that if your viewer clicks on the Cricut machine and enters the Amazon site but bought something else that interests him or her, you will still be paid on your viewer's purchase. This is why I suggest that you should not only have an affiliate program with the Cricut Company only; you should also have an affiliate link with Amazon.

Chapter 4.
Tips and Tricks

H acks, tips, and techniques—call it what you want, but every Cricut crafter needs to know them to make crafting much easier, faster, and fuss-free. We will explore the many hacks regarding tools and supplies organizing, how to get the most out of your purchases, how to save time and money, and much more.

Use the Right Blade

Many vinyl cutting machines have various blades. The variety of Cricut blades includes, for example, the perfect point blade, the deep-sliced blade, and the rotating blade.

For each material you cut, you want to use the right blade. It is also necessary to check that no pieces of paper or vinyl are attached to the cutter blade and that it is clean.

Blade Setting

When you cut vinyl with the blade put too low, the pattern with the area to be weeded would end up pulling away. So, if you slice too deeply, you will struggle with a carriage board!

The modification of the cutting machine to the right depth makes weaving much easier. Make sure the knob is switched to the right material configuration. If you are uncertain, do a test if your configurations are correct for the particular vinyl form you use.

How to Organize Cricut Supplies

Making your craft space organized, no matter how big or small is imperative. First things firsts:

Cricut Mat Organization

You will have plenty of mats for various crafting needs, and the more you continue your Cricut crafts, the more mats you'll have. So how do you keep them all organized? Hanging your mats on the wall according to the grip strength is one way. You can use basket storage or file storage, and you can even use command hooks to organize and sort your mats. Having them displayed on the wall will save you some time looking and searching for them.

Cricut Vinyl Rolls

One of the best ways to keep all your vinyl rolls perfectly organized is by using Ikea trash bag holders. Crafters swear by it. Just do a quick Google search, and you'll find plenty of images showing you how you can stack these rolls easily in the holders. The holders cost only about $10 or so, and they can hold up to 14 rolls each. Get a few of them and organize your rolls according to color and style.

Cricut Tools

For tools, you can use jars or canisters to keep your tools safely and securely. Some crafters also use $5 pegboards purchased from Target that have tiny holes in them that you can easily hang. Keeping them on pegboards prevents the nuisance of digging around for them. You get to see your tools displayed nicely, and there's no guessing where everything is. All your tools are within easy reach.

How to Quickly Weed Vinyl

Weeding is both satisfying and troublesome at the same time. Some crafters find joy in weeding out all the little cuts because it's really very satisfying to see your artwork coming together, but it is bothersome as well because weeding out takes time.

Whether you like to have vinyl or iron-on weeded, I'm sure these strategies will make your weeding quicker and less defective! Even the weeding of the most complex vinyl models can be made simpler with these techniques. Such tips of vinyl weaving refer to all vinyl forms, whether iron-on vinyl or vinyl adhesive. These tips are particularly useful for weaving small numbers and letters or weaving complex mandala designs.

The best way to make this process fast is by using your Cricut Bright Pad. All you need to do is place your craft on the top of the lightbox, so the light peeks through all those intricate cut lines. You can see all these lines more visibly, and it also saves time because you do not need to guess where the cuts are. If the BrightPad is not within your budget, you can also place your vinyl on a window or a brighter area, so the light makes it easier for you to see.

Conventional irons have hot and cold spots that result in you taking more time to cover the surface of your iron projects to ensure that everything sticks on easily. But with the Easy Press has a large surface area, and the heating is distributed evenly on the entire surface, ensuring that your iron-on is safely and securely ironed on. You do not need to worry about burning your project because the temperature is too hot on one end while the other end doesn't even stick. When working with iron-on, look at the Cricut temperature chart to select the temperature that is appropriate for your craft and the time needed to press until the machine beeps.

How to Use Vinyl Scraps

Many crafters do not throw away their vinyl scraps because they can be used again. Plus, it helps if you use the scraps again to save the environment. One of the best ways to use scraps is to place them on your mat and use the Snap Mat feature found in the Cricut App. What this does is that it will take a photo of your mat and allows you to arrange your designs on the scraps so that they can be cut out perfectly. This means no more guesswork and no more waste. These scraps also work great with quilters working on fussy cuts on their fabric. You can use the Snap Mat features to take a photo of the fabric and the mat. Next, place these designs over the images you want to cut out.

Cricut Explore and Maker Pen Hack

Cricut has an amazing array of pens, and they always come up with new pen products to help you explore and enhance your creativity. Apart from using the Cricut markers, did you know that you can use any other sharpie or marker or colored pencil with your Cricut machine?

Best Piece of Vinyl to Use for Your Business and Personal Projects

Different vinyl manufacturers are churning out different products for craft, different colors, textures, and options. Be careful what piece of vinyl material you use for your project so that you do not ruin your project. Know the different types if you must work with the vinyl material or use the recommended one for your project.

Adhesive Vinyl

This is the most common vinyl material on the market. You will come across it regularly sometimes in your starter kit with your machine. It comes attached to a carrier sheet coated with silicone, and you can easily pull the vinyl off. Use transfer tape to transfer it to its final place on your project, that is, after it has been cut and weeded. There are two types of adhesive vinyl materials—removable and permanent.

Removable adhesive vinyl is the regular Cricut vinyl material mostly used for indoors, temporal outdoor events, or placed on any surface that will not touch regularly or in need of a wash (wall decal). If I suggest, I will go for Oracal 631. On the other hand, permanent adhesive vinyl is waterproof and lasts longer than temporal adhesive vinyl.

They are usually rated to last six years or more. Its application is in DIY projects that need regular washing like tumblers, shot glasses, exterior walls, car decals, and more.

Heat Transfer Vinyl

This is the type used for fabrics. It is designed to bond to the fabric when heat and pressure are applied to it. Several features can help you determine the best quality of heat transfer vinyl material—color, finish, ease of weeding, price, durability, and cut reliability. Unlike adhesive vinyl, heat transfer vinyl does not require transfer tape. I will suggest Siser EasyWeed Heat Transfer Vinyl as the best of the rest.

Cling Vinyl

This is a type of vinyl material with no adhesive attached to it but uses static electricity to attach to smooth surfaces like windowpanes and removable decorations on mirrors. It can be removed and reused again on dry and clean surfaces. I will suggest Grafix Cling Vinyl Film to you.

De-Tack Your Cutting Mat

Your Cricut Explore Air will arrive with a cutting mat upon which you will put your projects before cutting. When purchased newly, the cutting mat is usually very sticky. I would advise that you prime the cutting mat before your first use. Priming makes it less sticky such that your paper projects don't get damaged. You prime the cutting mat by placing a clean and dry fabric over the cutting stock, over the cutting mat, and pulling it out again.

Keep Your Cutting Mat Clean

Use wipes to keep your cutting mat clean. Be careful with alcohol wipes as they could make the mat lose stickiness. You can also use the plastic cover to store your cutting mat when it is not in use. Besides covering the mats, they also need proper cleaning. You can always throw the dirty ones and replace them with new ones until your mats turn non-sticky and greasy, clean with some cleaner. You can also use baby wipes to clean residue or grime on the mats.

Use the Proper Tools

Use the correct Cricut Tools. The best tools are the ones from the Cricut Tool Set. This toolset contains tweezers, scrapers, scissors, a spatula, and a weeding tool. These tools make work go very smoothly.

Start Your Cricut Journey With the Sample Project

It is best to start with the sample project and the material provided. The materials you will find in the package will be sufficient for you to start an initial sample project. Start with a simple sample project to have a feel of how the machine works.

Always Run Test Cuts

When carrying out projects, it is advisable to do a test cut before running the whole project. You can designate a simple cut to test run your settings before cutting material for the project. If the blade is not well set, the test cut will reveal it. This is important if you have never work with Cricut materials or using a new one. So, it's best to test the material by making a little cut on it, like a circle or a small heart. By this, you will see the quality of the material, and you will know if you have chosen the right one. And you don't have to waste the whole sheet.

Replace Pen Lids after Use

Replace the pen lids when you are done using your pens. This prevents it from drying out. It's a good thing that Design Space sends a notification that reminds you to put the lid back on!

Use Different Blades for Different Materials

Do not use one single blade for all the different materials you will cut. For example, you can have one blade for cardboard, another for only leather, and one for vinyl. It is best to have different blades for different materials because each material wears differently on the blade. A dedicated blade will be best because it will be tuned to the peculiarities of each material.

Use Weeding Boxes for Intricate Patterns

When cutting delicate or intricate patterns, it is important to use weeding boxes in the process. Create a square or recmat using the square tool in Cricut Design Space and place it such that all your design elements are in it. Doing this makes weeding easier as all your design elements are grouped within the square or recmat you have created. When you are weeding your projects, instead of leaving them in the working place, collect them in an emptied box like a tissue box. This will not only keep your craft space clean but will also prevent the vinyl pieces from sticking to everything else.

Always Remember to Set the Dial

This sounds like stating the obvious setting the dial to the right material is something you can easily forget. The consequences of forgetting to set the dial to the appropriate material range from damaged cutting mats to shallow cuts on the materials; you can prevent these by always setting the dial before cutting.

Keep Crafting Tools in One Place

Collect the crafting tools and keep them in one place. It could be a box in which you can clearly see the entire tool in one glance. Place it close to you so that they are easy to access when you need them. It saves you a lot of frustration when you are unable to find a certain tool and leave your project in the middle to hunt it in your craft room.

Cover Your Cutting Mats

Your Cricut mats come with a cover, so don't throw them away. Instead, use them to keep the mats dust-free and clean between crafting.

Use Sharpie Pens

Cricut pens are amazing for personalizing your project. But when they run out, you can use less expensive sharpie pens in their place. They work well in the Cricut.

Peel off the Mat With Gravity

To avoid curl in your Cricut paper projects, you need this hack! Peel the mat off your project by going with gravity, and you will see your paper project is perfectly straight.

Replace Scrapers With Gift Cards

Keeping scraper tools is a must in the craft room, but you may not find them close to you at times. Under this situation, reach out to your credit card and use it to smooth out the vinyl. You can also use old gift cards for this purpose.

Keep Painter's Tape Handy

You may want to wrap your hand when you are weeding. When you are weeding, you can stick the pieces to the tape, and in this way, they won't end up on all of your working space. This hack is great when you are working on big Cricut projects.

Chapter 5.
Step by Step Projects

Wooden Gift Tags
Supplies Needed:
- Balsa wood
- Gold vinyl
- Vinyl transfer tape
- Cutting mat
- Weeding tool or pick

Instructions:
1. Secure your small balsa wood pieces to the cutting mat, then tape the edges with masking tape for additional strength.
2. Open Cricut Design Space and create a new project.
3. Select the shape you would like for your tags and set the Cricut to cut wood, then send the design to the Cricut.
4. Remove your wood tags from the Cricut and remove any wood excess.
5. In Cricut Design Space, select the "Text" button in the lower left-hand corner.
6. Choose your favorite font, and type the names you want to place on your gift tags.
7. Place your vinyl on the cutting mat.
8. Send the design to your Cricut.
9. Use a weeding tool or pick to remove the excess vinyl from the text.
10. Apply transfer tape to the quote.
11. Remove the paper backing from the tape.
12. Place the names on the wood tags.

13. Rub the tape to transfer the vinyl to the wood, making sure there are no bubbles. Carefully peel the tape away.
14. Thread twine or string through the holes, and decorate your gifts!

Pet Mug

Supplies Needed:

- Plain white mug
- Glitter vinyl
- Vinyl transfer tape
- Cutting mat
- Weeding tool or pick

Instructions:

1. Open Cricut Design Space and create a new project.
2. Select the "Image" button in the lower left-hand corner and search for "cat," "dog," or any other pet of your choice.
3. Choose your favorite image and click "Insert."
4. Search images again for paw prints, and insert them into your design.
5. Arrange the pet and paw prints how you'd like them on the mug.
6. Place your vinyl on the cutting mat.
7. Send the design to your Cricut.
8. Use a weeding tool or pick to remove the excess vinyl from the design.
9. Apply transfer tape to the design.
10. Remove the paper backing, and apply the design to the mug.
11. Rub the tape to transfer the vinyl to the mug, making sure there are no bubbles.
12. Carefully peel the tape away.
13. Enjoy your custom pet mug!

Organized Toy Bins

Supplies Needed:

- Plastic toy bins in colors of your choice
- White vinyl
- Vinyl transfer tape
- Cutting mat
- Weeding tool or pick

Instructions:

1. Open Cricut Design Space and create a new project.
2. Select the "Text" button in the lower left-hand corner.
3. Choose your favorite font and type the labels for each toy bin. See below for some possibilities—legos, Dolls, Cars, Stuffed animals, Outside Toys.
4. Place your vinyl on the cutting mat.
5. Send the design to your Cricut.
6. Use a weeding tool or pick to remove the excess vinyl from the text.
7. Apply transfer tape to the words.
8. Remove the paper backing and apply the design to the bin.
9. Rub the tape to transfer the vinyl to the bin, making sure there are no bubbles.
10. Carefully peel the tape away.
11. Organize your kid's toys in your new bins!

Froggy Rain Gear

Supplies Needed:

- Matching green raincoat and rain boots
- White outdoor vinyl
- Vinyl transfer tape
- Cutting mat
- Weeding tool or pick

Instructions:

1. Open Cricut Design Space and create a new project.
2. Select the "Image" button in the lower left-hand corner and search for "frog."
3. Choose your favorite frog and click "Insert."
4. Copy the frog and resize. You will need three frogs, a larger one for the coat and two smaller ones for each boot.
5. Place your vinyl on the cutting mat.
6. Send the design to your Cricut.
7. Use a weeding tool or pick to remove the excess vinyl from the design.
8. Apply transfer tape to the design.
9. Remove the paper backing and apply the design to the coat or boot.
10. Rub the tape to transfer the vinyl to the rain gear, making sure there are no bubbles.
11. Carefully peel the tape away.
12. Dress your kid up to play in the rain!

Easy Envelope Addressing

Supplies Needed:

- Envelopes to address
- Cricut Pen Tool
- Lightstick cutting mat

Instructions:

1. Open Cricut Design Space and create a new project.
2. Create an appropriate size box for your envelopes.
3. Select the "Text" button in the lower left-hand corner.
4. Choose one handwriting font for a uniform look or different fonts for each line to mix them up.
5. Type your return address in the upper left-hand corner of the design.
6. Type the "to" address in the center of the design.
7. Insert your Cricut pen into the auxiliary holder of your Cricut, making sure it is secure.
8. Place your cardstock on the cutting mat.
9. Send the design to your Cricut.
10. Remove your envelope and repeat as needed.
11. Send out your "hand-lettered" envelopes!

Watercolor Heart Sign

Supplies Needed:

- Watercolor paper
- Watercolor paints and paintbrush
- Glue
- Lightstick cutting mat
- Weeding tool or pick
- Frame

Instructions:

1. Paint your watercolor paper in soft gradients. Use a lot of water and gradually blend two or three colors into each other. Set aside to dry.
2. Open Cricut Design Space, and create a new project.
3. Select the "Image" button in the lower left-hand corner and search for "heart."
4. Select the heart of your choice and click "Insert."
5. Place your watercolor paper on the cutting mat.
6. Send the design to your Cricut.
7. Remove the outer edge of the paper, leaving the heart on the mat.
8. Use your weeding tool or carefully pick to remove the heart from the mat.
9. Glue your heart to the center of a blank piece of paper, cut to fit your frame.
10. Place your sign into your frame.
11. Set or hang wherever you need a little color!

Patterned Gift Wrap

Supplies Needed:

- White kraft paper
- Cricut Pen Tool in color(s) of your choice
- 12x24 cutting mat
- Weeding tool or pick

Instructions:

1. Open Cricut Design Space and create a new project.
2. Select the "Image" button in the lower left-hand corner and search for doodled images appropriate for the gift you're wrapping, for example, "Christmas doodle" or "birthday doodle."
3. Select the images you like and click "Insert."
4. Copy, resize, and rotate the images to create a pattern you like for your wrapping paper's size
5. Change the doodle's colors if desired—leaving them black creates a coloring-book feel, or you can make them in different colors.
6. Place your paper on the cutting mat.
7. Send the design to your Cricut.
8. Remove your wrapping paper from the mat.
9. Wrap your gift in your customized wrapping paper!

Vinyl Chalkboard

Supplies Needed:

- Cricut Explore 2
- Standard Grip mat
- Cricut Linen vinyl in desired colors
- Weeder, transfer tape
- Chalkboard and chalk pen

Instructions:

1. Log into the "Design Space" application and click on the "New Project" button on the top right corner of the screen to view a blank canvas.
2. Click on the "Projects" icon and type in "Vinyl Chalkboard" in the search bar.
3. Click on "Customize" to further edit the project to your preference, or simply click on the "Make It" button and load the vinyl sheet to your Cricut machine. Using a Weeder tool, remove the negative space pieces of the design.
4. Use the transfer tape to apply the vinyl cuts to the chalkboard. Then use the scraper tool on top of the transfer tape to remove any bubbles, and then just peel off the transfer tape.
5. Lastly, use a chalk pen to write messages.

Vinyl Herringbone Bracelet

Supplies Needed:

- Cricut Maker or Cricut Explore
- Standard Grip mat
- Vinyl (midnight)
- Weeder
- Scraper
- Transfer tape
- Metal bracelet gold

Instructions:

1. Log into the "Design Space" application and click on the "New Project" button on the top right corner of the screen to view a blank canvas.

2. Click on the "Images" icon on the "Design Panel," and type in "#M33278" in the search bar. Select the image and click on the "Insert Images" button at the bottom of the screen.

3. Click on "Customize" to further edit the project to your preference, or simply click on the "Make It" button, load the vinyl sheet to your Cricut machine, and follow the directions on the screen to cut your project.

4. Using a weeder tool, remove the negative space pieces of the design. Use the transfer tape to apply the vinyl cuts to the bracelet. Then use the scraper tool on top of the transfer tape to remove any bubbles, and then just peel off the transfer tape.

Treasure Chest Jewelry Box

Supplies Needed:

- Plain wooden box with lid
- White vinyl
- Vinyl transfer tape
- Cutting mat
- Weeding tool or pick Small blade

Instructions:

1. Select the "Image" button in the lower left-hand corner and search for "keyhole."
2. Click your favorite keyhole design and click "Insert."
3. Select the "Text" button in the lower left-hand corner.
4. Choose your favorite font and type "Treasure."
5. Place your vinyl on the cutting mat.
6. Send design to Cricut.
7. Make use of a weeding tool or pick to remove the excess vinyl from the design.
8. Apply separate pieces of transfer tape to the keyhole and the word.
9. Remove the paper backing from the tape on the keyhole.
10. Place the keyhole where the lid and box meet so that half is on the lid and half is on the box.
11. Rub the tape to transfer the vinyl to the wood, making sure there are no bubbles. Carefully peel the tape away.
12. Use a sharp blade to cut the keyhole design in half so that the box can open.
13. Transfer the word to the front of the box using the same method.
14. Optionally, add details with paint or markers to make the box look more like a treasure chest. Add wood grain, barnacles, scashells, or pearls.
15. Store your jewelry in your new treasure chest!

Motivational Water Bottle

Supplies Needed:

- Sturdy water bottle of your choice
- Glitter vinyl
- Vinyl transfer tape
- Light grip cutting mat
- Weeding tool or pick

Instructions:

1. Measure the space on your water bottle where you want the text and create a box of that size.
2. Select the "Text" button in the lower left-hand corner.
3. Choose your favorite font and type the motivational quote you like best; I sweat glitter, Sweat is magic, I don't sweat, I sparkle.
4. Place the vinyl on the cutting mat.
5. Send the design to Cricut.
6. Use a weeding tool or pick to remove the excess vinyl from the text.
7. Apply transfer tape to the quote.
8. Remove the paper backing from the tape.
9. Place the quote where you want it on the water bottle.
10. Rub the tape to transfer the vinyl to the bottle, making sure there are no bubbles. Carefully peel the tape away.
11. Bring your new water bottle to the gym for motivation and hydration!

Customized Makeup Bag

Supplies Needed:

- Pink fabric makeup bag
- Purple heat transfer vinyl
- Cutting mat
- Weeding tool or pick
- Keychain or charm of your choice

Instructions:

1. Measure the space on your makeup bag where you want the design and create a box that size.
2. Select the "Image" button in the lower left-hand corner and search "monogram."
3. Choose your favorite monogram and click "Insert."
4. Place vinyl on the cutting mat.
5. Send the design to your Cricut.
6. Use a weeding tool or pick to remove the excess vinyl from the design.
7. Place the design on the bag with the plastic side up.
8. Carefully iron on the design.
9. After cooling, peel away the plastic by rolling it.
10. Hang your charm or keychain off the zipper.
11. Stash your makeup in your customized bag!

Pumpkin Pillows

Supplies Needed:

- Burlap pad spread
- Printable heat transfer
- Material paper (whenever required for your image)
- Iron
- Printer and ink
- Pumpkin files of your choice

Instructions:

1. Download the pumpkin files that you want to use to your PC as a jpg document. Use the transfer button in the configuration space to import. For the blue pumpkin particularly, make sure to pick the complex picture type. The other two imported fine with the reasonably complex setting.

2. When you add the picture to the canvas, you can see that it is a print, at that point, cut by the layer's menu on the right-hand side. Resize to whatever size you require for your pumpkin pillow. You should remember the size of your heat transfer. The Cricut will likewise print an outskirt around the picture to see it on the machine. It will have to be adjusted if the picture is too huge to even consider fitting with the fringe.

3. Press start and wait until it ready, and you can cut it. Ensure that the material size is right before you begin to heat transfer.

Cowhide Notebook

Supplies Needed:

- Cricut explore 2
- Blade
- Scoring Wheel
- Cricut Metallic Leather
- Foil Posterboard
- White cardstock (12×24 sheets offer better material usage)
- Regular Iron-on in white
- Material Paper
- Special blade
- Needle
- String
- Scissors
- Weeding tools (optional)
- Cricut EasyPress
- Simple Press mat
- Speedy dry glue
- Cricut Cut File

Instructions:

1. The sharp blade edge incredibly cuts cowhide spread. Make sure to move the star wheels right to one side before cutting.
2. For the Iron-on applique, make sure to reflect your picture before cutting. Cut with your fine point cutting edge and remove extra bits with your weeding instruments.
3. Cut nine white card stock pieces that are scored down the middle. The 12×24 size papers offer better material use here. The single scoring wheel works extraordinary for ordinary card stock. The machine will score your material first; at that point, stop and request the sharp cutting edge.

4. For foil card stock and this sort of material, the scoring wheel is an absolute necessity. Use the twofold wheel to guarantee an incredible overlap line with no breaking. You can change the scoring wheel from single to twofold effectively with the Quick-Swap Drive Housing.
5. Use the Easy Press for best performance.
6. Put the weeded bit of iron-on on the cowhide with the transporter sheet and keep everything joined.
7. Spread the whole thing with material paper to secure your surface.
8. Follow the guidelines of Cricut Easy Press rules for time and temperature.
9. Remove the transporter sheet while still warm.
10. At that point, use speedy dry glue to put the foil banner board within your scratchpad, as demonstrated. Line up the folds with the little cuts in the cowhide.
11. Simply pull up on the circle made in the calfskin and afterward get it through the rectangular opening. Include a pen, and this is one charming DIY cowhide diary! It makes for a beautifully customized gift.

PART 3.

CRICUT DESIGN SPACE

Chapter 1.
The Software Design Space

Design Space

Design Space is the design software that comes with every new Cricut cutting machine. There is a downloadable app for both desktop and mobile devices which can be used both offline and online. Most of the Cricut cutting machine models that came out in the last four to five years have Bluetooth connection capability. With the ability to connect wirelessly, the Cricut cutting machines can be used with iOS and Android devices. They are also compatible with MAC and Windows systems through both Bluetooth as well as USB connectivity.

The first few models of the Cricut cutting machines came with their own screens, keyboards, and graphic cartridges. They did not need a design package to create various crafts. Although they were remarkable craft machines for their time, they also had limited crafting and cutting abilities.

The latest model of Cricut machines have more advanced capabilities with a streamlined design that allows for more cutting space and a wider range of cutting materials. They no longer have a built-in screen or keyboard. Models like the Cricut Maker and Cricut Joy no longer come with a cartridge slot either. They rely entirely on the Design Space image, project, and font libraries to function. Design Space gives the crafter more control over their crafting projects. The software comes loaded with a library containing thousands of images. The software also includes hundreds of already created projects that can be customized to suit the crafter's needs. Design Space gives the user control over their projects, and as such, they are not limited to what is on a cartridge. The

Design Space image, fonts, templates, and project libraries are also frequently updated. Design Space is easy to learn and use. It is free to download and comes with free images, templates, fonts, and shapes. Design Space does require the user to create an ID to log in. This login ID allows users to save projects as well as images, fonts, or ready-made projects they may have purchased. Most of the machines come with a free trial membership to Cricut Access which gives its members access to free Cricut Access images, fonts, and projects. You do not have to be a Cricut Access member to buy any fonts, images, or projects. The beautiful thing about Design Space is that you can buy an individual image, font, or project as or when you need them.

How to Download Cricut Design Space

Visit **design.cricut.com,** and you will be required to log in or create a username and password. Register your details on the website, and make sure you write down your login details in case you log out in the future. Once you have taken care of that, click on a new project on the top right of the screen. This action will alert you to download the Design Space plugin. When the download process is complete, you will have to open the file, depending on your computer or browser. If you are using a Chrome browser, it will be on your download bar, located at the bottom. Click to open and click run or next, as prompted.

Follow all the download prompts. You will have to accept the terms and conditions and click install. The procedure is straightforward, and the prompts will walk you through everything. Finally, Design Space is downloaded, and it's time to explore. Before your machine can cut out projects, you will have to create your designs inside Design Space (also called Design Space canvas).

On the canvas, you will use the menu on the left side to kick off your designs.

- You will click upload to upload SVG files or images that you intend to cut. SVG is the abbreviation for Scalable Vector Graphic, and it is the most used file for cutting designs because it is explicit. SVG files can be found anywhere; you can find them on blogs, Etsy, and other places.

- The next menu on the left is Shapes. You can make use of stars, squares, circles, and other shapes to make your design. If you intend to make scorecards or do other paper projects, you'll find score lines here.

- The third item on the left menu is text. You can do several things with text, including; curving texts, making monograms, and using your personal fonts.

- The fourth item on the menu is Images. If you click the images icon, you will be redirected to the designs you can use if you are subscribed to Cricut Access or the designs you can buy from Cricut if you have no subscription.

- The fifth on the left menu is Projects. If you click on projects, you will see a display of projects that are up for sale. However, there is another dropdown menu that you can use to select your projects. Your saved projects are also located in that area.

- The sixth item on the left menu is Templates. Some crafters do not use this feature, but you can use templates to ascertain the size of the design you intend to cut and how it is meant to look on a shirt or apron. Mind you; it is used as a guide; thus, the actual template won't be cut out.

- The seventh on the left menu is the New+ button. If you want to start a new project, this is the menu to click. Always save your current project if you intend to keep it before starting a new one. The save button is located at the top right corner.

Understanding the Design Space Application

Cricut" is poised to become a one-stop-shop for all your crafting and DIY project ideas. Their "Design Space" application is developed to let the artist inside you flourish into the world of technological advancements. It is a free and easy-to-learn design software that can work with all kinds of "Cricut" devices. It is also a cloud-based application, which allows you to seamlessly access all your design files from any device whenever you need them.

Cricut Design Space is a companion application that supports designing and cutting with "Cricut Explore" and "Cricut Maker" machines. You will be able to start a project from scratch or choose from a wide variety of images, fonts, and ready to print designs of "Make it Now" projects.

The software is synchronized across your devices so you can start a project on your mobile phone when the inspiration strikes and pick it right up from your laptop. It also supports the integrated camera on your devices so you can view your designs on real-life backgrounds. You can then wirelessly connect the "Design Space" with your "Cricut Explore" or "Cricut Maker" to easily print and cut your designs.

You can create an account on "Cricut" for free and sign in with your "Cricut ID" to work on your fonts, pictures, and projects. It would even let you easily pay for any purchase made on "Cricut.com" or directly within "Design Space."

The "Cricut" machines and "Design Space" support Bluetooth connectivity so you can wirelessly connect the software with your machines. However, some machines may require a "wireless Bluetooth adapter" that you can easily purchase online.

Creating an Account on "Cricut.com"

Let's look at how you can get your own "Cricut ID" to log into the "Design Space" application. On the official "Cricut" site, select "**Design**" from the top right corner of the screen. A new window will open; from the bottom of the screen, select **"Create a Cricut ID."** Now, in the window, as shown in the picture below, you would need to enter your personal information, such as first name, last name, email ID, and password.

You would then need to check the box next to "**I accept the Cricut Terms of Use**" and click on "**Create a Cricut ID**." You will be instantly taken to the "Design Space" landing page and a message reading "**New! Set your machine mode**" will be displayed. With the steps above, you have registered your email address as your new "Cricut ID"!!!!

Now, let's see how you can complete your registration and start using "Design Space." When you log into "Design Space" for the first time, your screen will display the message as shown in the picture below.

Click on **"Next,"** as displayed in the picture above; a blacked-out screen with **"Machine"** on the top right corner of the screen will be displayed as shown in the picture below.

Click on **"Machine,"** and the options of the "Cricut" machines will be displayed as shown below.

You can select your device from the two options. For this example, "Cricut Maker" was selected, and upon selection, the next screen will confirm the device you selected, as shown in the picture below.

Remember, if you wish to toggle to the "Cricut Explore," all you have to do is click on the "Maker," and you will see the dropdown option for the two machines again, as shown in the picture below.

Design Space on Mobile Devices

The "Design Space" is a cloud-based application, and you can pick up your project across various platforms. Here's how you can download the latest version (v 3.18.1) of this application on your mobile devices.

- From the Apple App Store (iOS), simply search for "Cricut" on the App Store from your iPhone or iPad and select "GET" to begin the download. You can then easily login with your registered "Cricut ID" to continue working on your projects on your phone.

- From Google Play (Android), you can search for "Cricut" on Google Play from your android phone and tablet. Then select "Install" to begin the download. Once completed, use your "Cricut ID" to login and pick up your projects and ideas where you left off.

"Design Space" Canvas

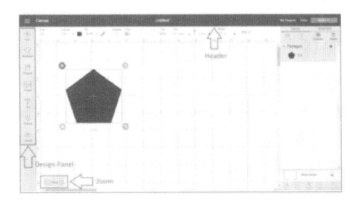

Think on the "Design Space" canvas as your playground where you can turn your ideas into reality. You will be able to create new projects, add images and/or texts to your existing projects and continue editing them until you are happy with the results.

So here is an overview of different elements of the "Design Space" canvas, as shown in the picture below:

Design Panel

- **New:**
  To start building a new project, you must always click on the "New" tab.

- **Templates:**
  To view your final design in the real-life background, you can use any of the relevant templates by clicking on the "Templates" tab.

- **Projects:**
  To search, select and cut designs from an already existing project, you can use the "Projects" tab, which will contain a variety of other projects along with your own projects.

- **Images:**
  The "Cricut Image Library" contains a wide variety of pictures available at your fingertips for free and to buy. The "Images" tab will also contain any image that you may upload.

- **Text:**
  You can use the "Text" tab to add desired phrases or words directly to the Canvas.

- **Shape:**
  You can use the "Shape" tab to insert simple shapes square, recmat, triangle, circle, and score lines into your Canvas.

- **Upload:**
  You can use the "Upload" tab to use your own image files, including jpg, gif, png, BMP, SVG, and dxf, at no charge.

Header

- **Menu:** The "hamburger" icon on the top left of the screen will allow you to navigate your "Cricut Design Space." You can directly access "Home," "Canvas," and several other "Design Space" features, such as "New Machine Setup," "Settings," "Link Cartridges," "Help," and "Sign Out."

  Page Title: This will help you remember whether you are on the "Home" or "Canvas" page of "Design Space." By clicking on the "Page Title," you will be able to close an open tab.

- **Project Name:** This will show you the name of your project. If you've not already saved your project, then "Untitled" will be displayed as the name of the project.

- **My Projects:** You can open your saved projects by clicking on "My Projects."

- **Save:** To access your projects across your devices and multiple platforms, you must save your projects to your account by clicking on the "Save" icon and providing a name for your projects. As a note, if you would like to keep your project private and all to yourself, then make sure you uncheck the "Public" option while saving your project. Once the project has been saved and you would like to rename your project, just click on "Save As" and enter a new name for your project.

- **Make it:** Click on the "Make It" icon when you have prepped your mats and are ready to transfer your project to your "Cricut" machine.

Zoom

You can "Zoom In" to look at the finer details of your project and "Zoom Out" to see an overview of the same.

Activity Selection

To start the project on Design Space, "Cricut" cutting machines are capable of doing more than just cut when used in conjunction with "Design Space" and other "Cricut" tools and accessories. As mentioned earlier, within "Design Space," each of these activities, namely "Cut, Draw, Score, Engrave, Deboss, Perf, and Wavy," are called "Linetype."

When you are ready to start designing your project, the first step is to identify which "Linetype" applies to you and make the appropriate selection as shown in the steps below:

- Login to "Design Space" and make sure that your machine selection is correct. Then select "New Project," either on the top right corner of the screen or from the landing page, as shown in the picture below.

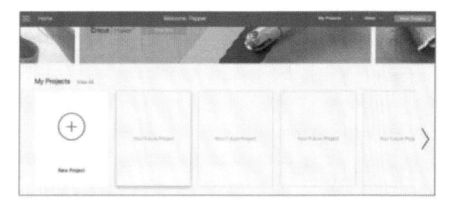

- As a note, for the first-time users, you will be displayed a message to download the "Design Space" plugin for your system. Click on download to download the zip file. Once the download has started, you will see the message below on your screen. To install the plugin, enter your computer's administrator ID and password and follow the prompts. Do not confuse this with your "Cricut ID."

- Once the installation has finished, the message as shown in the picture above will disappear, and you will be able to access the blank canvas. On the blank canvas as shown in the picture below, click on the image's icon, and a list of free and for purchase images available through the "Design Space" image library will open. You can also select text by clicking on the text icon and follow the steps below. Select an image that best meets your needs and click on "Insert Images" at the bottom of your screen, as shown in the picture below.

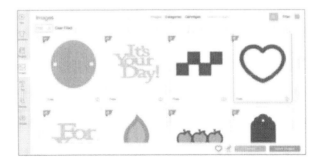

Your selected image will be loaded onto the canvas, and the tools panel on top of the screen will become active in black fonts. On the top left corner of the screen, click on "Linetype" and select the activity that fits your project. Based on your "Linetype" selection, the image will be modified to reflect the change, and once you are ready to transfer your project to the machine, "Design Space" will guide you to mount the appropriate tool in the machine.

Cricut Access Subscription Frequent Problems and Solutions

The best part about these machines is that you can use them even though you are not that creative. In fact, there are plenty of Cricut users who are not very skilled in drawing or graphic design. Well, this brand has figured it out for them also, as all these users can get access to already made designs. They only need to add their personal touch. All of these wouldn't be possible without the Cricut Access subscription. But to find out what this service really entails, you will need to keep reading.

When you register, you will be prompted to fill in your name, email (Cricut ID), country, and a unique password. You will need to accept the Terms of Use to receive exclusive offers and inspiration.

If you truly want to make the most out of the Design Space application, you need the Cricut Access subscription. When setting the Cricut ID, you will choose your subscription plan, either monthly, annual, or premium. After this step, you should be able to select the "Maybe later" option to benefit from the Cricut Access free trial.

When you are just starting with Cricut, perhaps you are only interested in the fonts, and you would like to have access to such fonts. If you are looking just for fonts, don't worry! Cricut has you covered with the special Fonts membership. You have a monthly option of $6.99 or the annual version of $4.99 per month and paid in a lump sum. This membership covers access to 400 amazing fonts, but also the Priority Member Care line option.

If you want to have access to images, you won't settle for this subscription plan. In this case, you will choose the Standard Membership, which can be billed monthly at $9.99 or annually at $7.99 per month. This option will get you access to the 400 fonts, but also to 30,000 premium Cricut images, including some beautiful designs unique to the brand. But wait, that's not all! You will also get a 10% discount on ready-to-make projects, images, and licensed fonts or a 10% discount on product purchases from the Cricut Shop (machines, tools, materials, accessories, and many more). It goes without saying that the Priority Member Care line option is included. Pretty neat, right?

There is a subscription plan that can offer even more than that. Sounds interesting? This is the Premium Membership, and it can only be billed annually. It has a monthly value of $9.99, and it already has the features included by the previous subscription plans, but also some extra features:

- Unlimited access to more than 400 amazing fonts

- More than 30,000 premium Cricut images or designs

- Discounts on ready-to-make projects, images, or licensed fonts

- Discounts on purchases from the Cricut Shop, including materials, tools, accessories, machines, and more

- Discounts on designer images, fonts, or ready-to-make projects

- Free shipping on orders over a certain amount

- Priority Member Care line option

Bear in mind that you will need to invest more than the value of the machine to truly find out what your Cricut machine can do for you. This is what these subscription plans are for. Besides feeling the need to access several designs, fonts, or images, you may need to purchase accessories, tools, or materials from the Cricut Shop. The benefits you get with a Cricut Access subscription can only be used in the Cricut Shop when purchasing different items from the store, and they can't be used when purchasing from a retailer. These subscription plans do well to add loyal buyers to the Cricut Shop. Now that you have all the benefits and numbers of these subscription plans, which one best suits you? Or, how much are you willing to spend on a monthly or annual basis to get the most out of Cricut? As you can see, there isn't that much difference between these subscription plans, and they are quite affordable. Why not go Premium?

The subscription plan you choose should be based on your needs and annual budget. If you are looking to work on many projects, the Premium membership is the best option for you.

Chapter 2.
How to Get Started With a Project

Before you begin, download the desktop version of Cricut Design Space. In the application you can load images of various types: .jpg, .gif, .bmp, .svg or .dxf. For the non-vector images, if they are in a single color, we will have no problem when editing them to cut; if it is a png, nothing should be done as the program automatically detects the outline. If it is a .jpg, we will have to remove everything that is in the background.

It is very simple when what we want to cut is a single color, since in that case, with the magic wand, we would eliminate the background and READY TO CUT! But what do we do when the image we want to use is in various colors? In this case, we will have to create several files to be able to separate them, and it is a somewhat more complex process. But let's not be alarmed; in this post, we are going to make a multi-color image step by step to see the process that we should follow with a .jpg image.

Open a New Project and Load an Image

This is the main Design Space window when you open it. To start, we select New project. When we click on New Project, our workspace opens, there we select Upload

This screen will open where it tells us the types of files that can be uploaded; as we said at the beginning of this post, we are going to upload a JPG image. To load the image, we can search for it on our PC or drag it into the window that appears.

Image Edit to Remove Background and Separate Colors

Once we have our image loaded, we select its complexity, as it is an image with a lot of colors, and so that it detects all the detail, we select the Complex mode. If the image were a silhouette or two or three colors, we could select the Simple mode.

To start editing our image, we select the magic wand. Using it, we can erase with a single click a mass of the same color. In this case, we have eliminated the entire background at once

If we select the preview button, we can see the contour that it detects to crop. As you can see, we would do the whole drawing in a single cut, so we need to separate the colors.

With the help of the eraser, we can eliminate the elements that we do not want to cut. In this step, we are making the black layer first. You have to check from time to time with the option "Preview" that we do not have any element that we do not want.

When we have our finished color layer, we select Continue; in the next window, we will get two types of saving modes—To print and cut (if we want to print the complete drawing and then cut only the silhouette) or as a Cut Image, we will save like this since we will use it to do a project with textile vinyl.

Then we repeat the whole process of uploading the image and editing it with all the colors we want. Once we have all of them uploaded, we select them and click Insert Images to be able to load them in our workspace.

Editing the Image on the Worktable

When we have our files loaded in the workspace so that when cutting, we automatically have it separated by colors, we will assign a color to each of the layers.

And we already have our project ready to cut! If the work is for textiles and has text, you have to remember to mirror it so that when ironing, it is legible.

Chapter 3.
The Setting for Windows Mac and Android

Downloading and Installing Design Space

To access the Design Space software for a computer or mobile device, you will need an active internet connection.

Downloading and Installing Design Space for Windows

- The download is run from https://design-beta2.cricut.com/#/launcher.

- Choose Download to start the Design Space for Desktop download.

- When the system is downloading, the screen will prompt "Downloading Design Space for Windows." This can take a few minutes, depending on the connection and your device.

- Once the download is complete, go to the Downloads folder on the PC and double click on the file—Cricut Design Space Install v4.2.4.exe (the version number may differ depending on the updated version).

- There may be a pop-up window asking for permission to trust the application—select to trust the application, or it will not install.

- Follow any on-screen prompts, selecting the default settings until the software starts to install.

- During the installation, there will be a pop-up box with an installation progress bar to show how far the installation has progressed.

- Once the installation is complete, you will be asked to "Sign in with your Cricut ID."

- First-time users of the software will need to create a Cricut ID by clicking on the button below the sign-in sheet on the screen.

- The Cricut desktop icon automatically gets added to the Windows desktop or can be found under the "All Programs" taskbar where you find your installed programs.

- To access Cricut Design Space, click on either the desktop icon or the program under the All Programs taskbar.

Downloading and Installing Design Space for MAC

- The download is run from https://design-beta2.cricut.com/#/launcher.

- Choose the option to Download.

- When the system is downloading, the screen will prompt "Downloading Design Space® for MAC." This can take a few minutes, depending on the connection and your device.

- Once the download is complete, go to the Downloads folder on the MAC and double click on the file—Cricut Design Space Install v4.1.6 (the version number may differ depending on the updated version).

- When the Cricut icon appears, drag it into the applications folder, and the installation will begin.

163

- Once the installation is complete, you can drag the application icon to the dock to create a shortcut or access the program from the application folder.

- The first time you use Cricut on a MAC, you may get a warning "Cricut Design Space is an app downloaded from the internet. Are you sure you want to open it?"— Click on the Open button to continue to Design Space.

- On the first Design Space screen that appears, you will be asked to "Sign in with your Cricut ID."

- First-time users of the software will need to create a Cricut ID by clicking on the button below the sign-in sheet on the screen.

- To access Cricut Design Space, click on either the desktop icon or the program under the Applications folder.

Uninstall on Mac

- Go to Finder and open the Applications folder.

- Search for Cricut Design Space.

- Drag it to trash.

- Right-click on the Trashcan and select Empty Trash.

- It is recommended that you restart your computer after uninstalling any program from it before reinstalling any other program.

Downloading and Installing Design Space for iOS

- On an iOS compatible device, you will need to go to the App Store.

- In the Search option, find the Cricut Design Space app.

- To download and install the app, select Get. You may have to verify the download depending on your iTunes setup.

- When the app has finished downloading and installing, you will be directed to the "New Machine Setup" page. If you do not wish to go through the setup right away, you can either go to the app overview screen or click on the X in the top right-hand corner to exit.

- You can access the Cricut app by clicking on the application icon on your iOS mobile device.

Uninstall the Cricut Design Space

- Press and hold the Design Space icon until it vibrates.

- Press the X button to delete it from your device.

- Note that if you have saved projects on your device and not on the cloud, uninstalling will delete those projects. The recommended thing to do is to offload the app instead of saving your projects on your device.

Downloading and Installing Design Space for Android

- On an Android device, you will have to access the Google Play Store to get the Design Space app.

- In the Search box, find the Cricut Design Space app.

- To download and install the app, select Install, and the application will start to download.

- When the app has finished downloading and installing, you will be directed to the "New Machine Setup" page. If you do not wish to go through the setup right away, you can either go to the app overview screen or click on the X in the top right-hand corner to exit.

- You can access the Cricut app by clicking on the application icon on your Android mobile device.

Uninstall App on Android

- Go to the Settings app.

- Tap "Apps" or "Applications."

- Swipe to the "Download" tab or "Application Manager."

- Navigate to the App you intend to uninstall.

- Tap the "Uninstall" button.

Connecting the Cricut to Your Computer

- Now, you can turn on your machine.

- To connect the unit that requires the cable to your laptop, you simply have to put the square end in its designated place at the back of your Cricut and attach the rectangular end to the USB port on your desktop or laptop.

- If you have a wireless device, enable your Bluetooth on whichever device you wish to connect your Cricut to, open the Bluetooth settings, and pair with the machine. You will instantly recognize the name of your machine.

- Design Space will automatically pick up your operating system when you first download it.

- Design Space remembers your login details, so you will not have to enter them every time you log in. You can opt not to use this option if you prefer to log in every time.

- You should save your work regularly when working in the application as it does not have an auto-save feature.

Chapter 4.
Which Printer to Choose and What Features It Should Have

Design Space has launched the new Design Space for Desktop. As this is new, there are still a few bugs and updates that Design Space will roll out shortly, which is why it's called Desktop Beta.

Desktop Beta Differences

- Design Space Desktop can now be run directly from the Desktop and does not require the user to log in from the Design Space website. This makes Design Space available in offline mode without an internet connection.

- The Desktop Design Space application gives the user the ability to save their projects both on their PC and keep them in the cloud. This makes working with your favorite projects easy both offline and online.

- Images can now be downloaded for offline use, as can projects and fonts.

Downloading Design Space Desktop Beta

Downloading Design Space Desktop Beta requires an active internet connection.

Minimum System Requirements for Design Space

Design Space is compatible with Windows, MAC, iOS, and Android operating systems. To run the software on these systems, devices must meet the following minimum system requirements:

Windows Operating Systems

- Microsoft Windows version 8 or higher

- The device must have Bluetooth or USB support

- The CPU should be either Intel Dual-Core or AMD processor of equivalent specifications

- The device must have at least 4GB of RAM

- The device must have at least 2GB of free disk space

- The screen display should be able to support a resolution of at least 1024px x 768px

MAC Operating Systems

- MAC OS 10.12 or higher

- The device must have Bluetooth or USB support

- The CPU should be at least 1.83 GHz

- The device must have at least 4GB of RAM

- The device must have at least 2GB of free disk space

- The screen display should be able to support a resolution of at least 1024px x 768px

iOS

- iOS 11 or higher

- iPhones from the iPhone 5s and newer models

- iPad mini 2 and newer models

- iPad Air and newer models

- iPad Pro 12.9" and new models

- iPad 5th generation

- iPod touch 6th generation

Android

- Android 6.0 or higher

- Mobile devices

- Tablets

- Chromebooks are not compatible

Design Space Softwares

There are several options for design software that can be used with the Cricut machines. Each one has its own advantages and disadvantages. Knowing which one fits best for your needs is determined by what you would like to use it for.

Below, we will explore the different design systems and software and which devices work best with these different software programs.

The Cricut Design Space is best used for the:

1. Cricut Explore One

2. Cricut Explore Air 2

3. Cricut Explore

4. The Cricut Maker

5. Cricut Explore Air

6. Cricut Design Space

Cricut Design Space is used with an internet connection to be used efficiently. It provides an easy way of creating designs for your crafting and DIY needs. The only downside is that it cannot be used on a Chromebook computer, so you will need to use a standard iOS, Android, or Microsoft device. Besides, it has a cloud-based service; you can start your design process in your account on one device and transfer it to another to finish the design.

Once you purchase or create an image, you will be able to have access to that image in your library for lifetime use. There is a provided format for joining words with images; however, once these are saved as an attached file, you cannot separate them. So, it is better that you have the individual files saved separately for later individual use.

Cricut Basic

This is a program or software designed to help the new user get an easy start on designing new crafts and DIY projects. This system will help you with image selection to cutting with the least amount of time spent in the design stages. You can locate your image, pre-set projector font, and immediately print, cut, score, and align with tools that are found within the program.

You can use this program on the iOS 7.1.2 or later systems as well as iPad and several of the iPhones from the Mini to the 5th generation iPod touch. Since it is also a cloud-based service, you are able to start on one device and finish from another.

Cricut Sync

This is a program designed for updating the Cricut Expression 2, as well as the Imagine machine and the Gypsy device. You just connect your system to the computer and run the synced program for an update installation on the features that come with your machine. This is also used to troubleshoot any issues that could arise from the hardware.

Make the Cut

This is a third-party program that works with the Cricut design software. It offers a straightforward look at the design features that Cricut has. This system can convert a raster image into a vector so that you can cut it. There is also a great way to do lattice tools. It uses many file formats and TrueType fonts. There are advanced tools for editing and an interface that is easy to learn and use. This system works with Craft ROBO, Gazelle, Silhouette, Wishblade, and others. It allows you to import any file from a TTF, OTF, PDF, GSD, and convert them to JPG, SVG, PDF, and so on. It is flexible and user-friendly.

Sure Cuts a Lot

This is another third-party software that has a funny name, which gives you the ability to take control of your designs without some of the limitations that can happen when using cartridges used within the Cricut Design Studio. You will need to install an update to your software to use this program; you can download it for free. It allows for the use of TrueType and OpenType font formats as well as simple drawing and editing tools. Also, you can import any file format and then convert it to the one that you need. There is an option for blackouts and shadows.

Cricut Design Studio

This program allows you to connect with your software and provides you with much more functionality, as far as shapes and fonts are concerned. There are various options for tools that provide you resources for designing more creative images. You will be able to flip, rotate, weld, or slant the images and fonts. However, you will still be limited in the amounts or types of fonts that you can use based on the ones on the cartridges. There is a higher level of software features that allow for customization.

Other accessories that you can use with the Cricut machines are blades, cartridges, and different cutting mats. Below, you will find a list of accessories that you can use for the Cricut machines. Each one of these accessories can be found at your local crafting store or online at the Cricut website. Each accessory has its own use and benefit. They come in a variety of options, colors, prices, and uses.

Essential Tools

The Cricut Tools Set is another optional accessory that could come in handy. This toolset will include a tweezer, spatula, scissors, scraper, weeder, and trimmer. Each one of these tools is useful in helping you with your crafting needs. Each one serves a purpose and provides you with endless options when creating with your Cricut.

Scoring Stylus

If you are looking to make a box or a card that folds or even anything else that has a precision edge that folds, then you will definitely need a scoring stylus. This makes scoring the edge much simpler. It fits into the housing with ease, and when using a library file from your design studio, it will not only create the design, but the scoring is built-in, making it easy to accomplish. This cuts your design and time in half. The cartridge is designed to hold the blade and the scoring tool at the same time.

Chapter 5.
Tips and tricks

Cricut Design Space Top Menu

To understand Cricut Design Space, let's explore the top menu.

- The top menu will only become available after you have texts typed out or a design uploaded. Thus, beginning from the left is the Undo button, used to rectify mistakes. The next button on the right is the Redo button, used to repeat an action.

- The Deselect button is next, and it is used as the opposite of select. The Edit button is next, and it has a dropdown menu that consists of copy or paste and flip. Next is the Size button; you can use it to change the actual size of your design or explore the bottom right of the design to use the two-way directional arrow.

- Right at the bottom left of the canvas is the unlock button. This feature consists of a four-way directional arrow used to widen designs without making them taller or making them taller with making them wider.

- Next on the menu is the rotation tool, used to rotate designs to every possible degree. The last feature on the top menu is the x and y coordinates, used to position designs on the canvas.

Working With Fonts in Design Space

One of the unique features of the Cricut Maker machine is the ability to personalize your project. This creative ability, innate in us, gives us maximum satisfaction and a great sense of accomplishment. Working with texts and fonts shows the unique freedom that the user of this machine has; the ability to show the power of creativity. As stated earlier, you can use the Cricut fonts or the one installed on your computer or device. So, how can you add text, select font, install/uninstall font in Windows/Mac? Let us take it one by one.

Add Text to Design Space

If you want to add text to canvas, you have to use the text tool on the canvas's left-hand side. Suppose you will locate the text at the bottom-left of the screen using IOS or android app. The text bar and text box will appear if you select the text tool in Windows or Mac. If you are using IOS or Android, the font list will open. After that, choose the font you intend to use and then type in your text. Note that you can type the text before selecting the font on a Windows/Mac computer. Select any area outside the text box to close it.

Double-tap or double-click on the text. To edit the text, you can choose the action you want, including font style, font size, change the font, letter spacing, and line spacing from the options available.

Editing Fonts

If you decided to add text to your design or select a "text object" on the Canvas or select a "text layer" in the Layers Panel, the "Text Edit Bar" will be displayed directly below the image "Edit Bar" on your screen. All the functions that can be seen on the "Text Edit Bar" are shown in the picture and explained below.

- **Font:** This will provide you a list of "Cricut" fonts along with all the fonts available on your computer.

- **Font Drop Down:** You will be able to view all the fonts available to you or may choose to view just the "Cricut" fonts, or only fonts installed on your system, or all the fonts at the same time, using the "Font DropDown." Font filters may also be searched and applied. Just browse the font list and choose your desired font to be applied to the selected text.

- **Font Filter:** You can use this feature for filtering the fonts by category and alter the fonts that are displayed in the "Font Type" menu.

- **All Fonts:** To view all available fonts that can be used for your project

- **System Fonts:** To view only the fonts installed on your system

- **Cricut Fonts:** To view just the fonts from the "Cricut" library

- **Single Layer Fonts:** To view fonts containing only a single layer

- **Writing Style Fonts:** To view fonts that are designed particularly to be written by hand. These fonts are characterized by letters with a single stroke that makes them appear like handwritten letters.

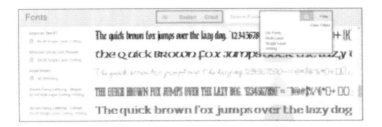

- **Style:** This feature will allow you to select the style of your font, such as "regular, bold, italic, and bold italic." You may also see the option of "writing" when an applicable font has been selected. Remember, the style of "Cricut" fonts may differ from your system fonts.

- **Font Size:** You can adjust the size of the fonts by typing in the desired point size or using the "stepper" to gradually adjust the font size by 1 point.

- **Letter Space:** You may want to adjust the spacing between letters of your text by typing in the desired value or using the "stepper."

- **Line Space:** If you need to adjust the spacing between individual rows of text, just type in the desired value or use the "stepper."

- **Alignment:** You can also modify the alignment of the entire block of text to one of these options: "left, right, centered, or full justification."

- **Curve:** You can enhance your text by bending it into a circular shape using the "Curve" feature and changing the diameter to your desired length.

- **Advanced:** The features in the "Advanced" tool will allow you to ungroup text contained within a block of text. This includes a grouping of individual letters as well as lines and layers of text.

- **Ungroup to Letters:** This feature will enable you to ungroup letters within a text and create individual layers for every letter.

These letters will then be displayed in the "Layers Panel," where you can modify the size and position of each letter independently while keeping the layers of these letters grouped together.

- **Ungroup to Lines:** You will be able to ungroup rows of text within a text box, and every line will be in a group of its own layers and will be displayed in the "Layers Panel" as an image that can be modified independently.

How to Upload Images With a Cricut Machine

The capacity to upload your own images into Design Space can be a lifesaver, particularly in the event that you can't discover anything remotely like what you're attempting to make. You can upload anything going from a PNG to a multilayered vector document, and Cricut will naturally process it. You will have the option to print, cut, or draw them any way you wish!

After you pick a fundamental image to upload, you will have the option to see the see and select the image to use. Basic images are fundamental and little documents that contrast hues with a strong foundation. Respectably perplexing images have more detail and shading, which you can see by look over them in Design Space.

Complex Images are definite and mix hues, so it is hard to tell the foundation from a closer view. Fluctuating degrees of concealing and mixing are remembered for this option. You will doubtlessly need to choose this version to do the most nitty-gritty crafting project.

The Scalable Vector Graphics SVG is the best when using your Cricut machine. They take into consideration more exact cuts than a PNG or JPG record. If you download an SVG document from the web, ensure you extract the SVG record on the off chance that it is downloaded as a ZIP record (.ZIP documents can't be uploaded into Design Space).

As a bonus tip, Google the realistic image you are looking for. SVG allows you to search the entirety of the accessible designs that you can bring into Cricut Design Space. Download the SVG file and upload it into Design Space if you can't discover what you're searching for on Cricut's base.

Browse the records you have on your PC or distributed storage and discover the image that you might want to upload.

Fundamental Image Upload

1. Upload the record you might want to import to Cricut Design Space. This will probably be a.JPG or.PNG record type. Next, open the document selector or drag the record into the upload section of Design Space.

2. You will, at that point, be able to choose Simple, Moderately mind-boggling, or Complex design types. Select the most pertinent and precise sort at that point; click "Continue."

3. Identify the cutting lines of the uploaded image. Make sure to use the Tools on the left of the Canvas, for example, Select, Erase, and Crop. If you see a checkerboard design behind your image that implies the zone has been removed successfully.

4. Click on Preview to see the cut lines of the uploaded image. On the off chance that you have to change the outcome, click Hide Preview to return and modify (from the past advance). Click Continue once you are prepared to proceed onward.

5. Name and label your image so you can discover it in your uploaded documents later. Either select "Print Then Cut" or "Cut image" to show what kind of action you might want your Cricut Machine to take. This will decide how the record is spared and ready to be used.

6. Finally, save the image. You will presently have the option to access and use your uploaded image.

Vector Image Upload

1. Select the .SVG document you might want to import to Cricut Design Space. Either intuitive or physically select and import the image from your PC documents.

2. Name the image appropriately so you can think that it's later.

3. The new image document will appear in the Uploaded Images Library at the base of the screen.

4. Vectors will appear on Canvas as an assembled image. You can ungroup them on the right-hand side of the canvas if necessary.

Essential Images

Essential images are JPG, BMP, PNG, and GIF records. For the most part, these are made in programs that work in pixels, similar to Adobe Photoshop.

Vector Images

Vector images are SVG and DXF document types. These documents will be naturally isolated into layers after uploading and sparing. These are, for the most part, made in programs that work in vectors, similar to Adobe Illustrator. Both of these strategies work, yet I regularly discover my Illustrator records are the best because the Cricut was designed to cut vector documents, so it peruses them locally. Be that as it may, don't stress; it cuts other pixel-based documents well!

Uploading a Basic File (Jpg) to the Cricut Design Space

I figured the ideal approach to disclose this is taking a gander at the procedure for cutting a similar image as an essential image and as a vector image. I made this straightforward shirt decal in Adobe Illustrator. I spared it as an SVF and as a JPG. Here's the procedure for uploading each:

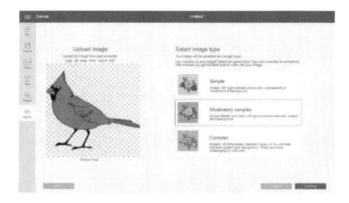

Start by clicking "Upload Image" on the left-hand menu, and explore the record you need to open. At that point, select it from the rundown of uploaded images and click "Supplement Images."

The Cricut Design Space will, at that point, ask you what type of image you are cutting. I generally select "tolerably complex image" since I think the product works somewhat harder to see the edges than with a straightforward image.

In the following screen, you'll select any piece of the design that is negative space—which means it doesn't get cut. You need to choose any white parts so they become straightforward (checked). Ensure you zoom in and choose the little regions of your project. Right now, it is needed to zoom in to click on the little design on the teepee and within the letters.

The last screen allows you to select whether this is a print-then-cut image or an ordinary cut image. Right now, only a Cut Image—no printing associated with this project. Once you are done, it will show up on your work screen. The files don't import at the right size, so you can modify that in the "alter" menu on the left. I zoomed in so you can perceive how the main file is only somewhat unpleasant around the edges. It will, in any case, cut and look incredible. However, a vector document is cleaner. Once you have your document, click GO in the upper right and cut your record!

Uploading Vector File (SVG) to the Cricut Design Space

The procedure for uploading a vector record is substantially more straightforward than uploading an essential document. Follow the instructions above to import your SVG. Once you find an "Images" button at a good pace, it will skip all the previous steps and import your image legitimately into the Cricut Design Space. On the off chance that you designed it at a specific size, those dimensions ought to be held when you import. At that point, click GO in the upper right, and you're high-tailing it!

How to Weld

It can be a little bit daunting for a Cricut Space beginner to use the weld tool. However, when you become proficient, it'll open the doors to many more projects because it is a tool that will be used often.

The weld tool is located at the bottom right corner of Design Space, under the layers panel. Other tools close to it are; flatten, contour, and slice tools.

In Cricut Design Space, the weld tool does the following;

- Connects cursive text and scrip for it to cut as a single word instead of individual letters

- Merge multiple layers and shapes into a single-layered image

- Take cut lines from different shapes and cut them as one big image

- To use weld, the text or shapes you intend to weld together must be touching or overlapping each other.

To select the layers you intend to weld together, select a layer, hold down "ctrl," and select the other layer. After selecting both layers, click "weld." If you intend to weld the whole layers on your canvas, click "select all" to select all the layers and click "weld."

If you weld different layers together, it becomes a single image and will cut out in one color and on one mat. Without selecting multiple layers, the weld option will not be available for use.

To weld texts, you have to make sure that the letters are all touching each other. Thus, you have to reduce the spacing of the letters until they begin to touch each other. Once you do this, you can select everything and click weld.

Chapter 6.
Project Step by Step

T he first thing that you need to do is go to Cricut.com. Then click Design; it is found at the top right corner. Once you have the right screen, you will be told that you need to sign in. Insert the needed information, and you will see that the email that you entered is going to be your identification, so you will need to remember which one you used. The next step that you will need to complete is when you hit the green button, you will be taken inside the app. This is where you begin doing your projects. Make sure to add this page to your toolbar by bookmarking it so that you can always find it when you need it.

Everyone's home screen on this looks a little different so keep that in mind. My projects for some people will come up first, so keep this in mind as well. Now, you have signed in, and you are ready to get started, so the first thing that you will do to start a new project is to click on the window that says Canvas. This is where you are going to do everything that you need for editing before you cut your projects.

The top panel of the app is for editing and arranging what you want in the canvas area. From here, you can choose the fonts you want, the size of the design, and more. The panel is divided into subpanels, and there are two of them that you will see. The first allows the user to name, save and cut your projects, while the second will enable you to control and edit things in the canvas area.

The first subpanel will allow you to navigate your canvas to your created profile or add it to the projects. It can also send the completed projects to cut. When you look at the toggle menu, you will see another menu that will slide open. This menu will come in handy, but that is not a part of the canvas, which is why it does not need too much detail—we will explain it anyway just to know what it is and how it works. The toggle menu lets you go to your profile and change the photo that you have chosen. There are other technical things that you can do from here as well, including the ability to calibrate your machine and its blade while also having the ability to update the Firmware software of your device.

You should explore the Design Space and look around so that you know everything and get comfortable with the app. When you look at the settings option that this offers, you will be able to change the measurements and the visibility of the canvas, and this is something that you will be able to use for a great benefit for your projects.

Suppose you need to re-cut a project you have previously created; this makes a great benefit; it is perfect if you do not want to recreate the same project repeatedly. From there, you will be able to have the save option, and it is recommended that you save your project as you go. This will help against your browser crashing.

Here's where you need to be specific. Different options are specific to the machine that you have. If you have, for example, a Maker, but you are designing with the options for Explore, you will realize that there is a multitude of things that you will not be able to do. There are also different options for the line type. When you are done uploading your files, you are ready to cut them on your canvas. Your projects will be divided into mats according to color.

The editing menu is extremely useful as it will help arrange or organize the fonts and images on the canvas. It will also help you edit it to make sure that it is exactly the way you want. You are going to make mistakes, and there are little buttons that can correct that for you in the form of two buttons—the undo or redo button. If you have created something you do not like, you can click the Undo button. You also have the option of line type and fill. With these options, you will be able to tell your machine what tools and blades to use. A great example is to remember that the Explore only cuts with three blades, and the Maker has six. The line type option tells your machine when you are going to cut and what tool to use as well as giving you seven options. If you have a Maker, every option will be available, but if you have an Explore, you only have three options available instead of seven. The first option that you will have is the Cut. This is the default, and every element on your canvas has this option. When you have selected Cut, you can change the fill of the elements, and it will translate into different colors of materials that you are going to use.

If you want to draw your designs, you can also do it when you select this. Instead of cutting, when you assign the Make It option, this will draw instead. This option does not color your designs.

The next option that you have is Score. When you assign this, all the designs will appear scored, or they will appear dashed. When you click Make It with this option, your cut will score whatever material you are using for these types of projects. You will need the scoring wheel or the scoring stylus for this. Keep in mind that the wheel only works if you have the Maker; it does not work with the Explore.

The last options are the perforation, the wavy, debossing, and engraving. They work with the quick swap adaptive also. If you already have one, you can just buy the tips. If you do not have one, then you can get them as well. They are relatively inexpensive, depending on how you purchase them. The fill option is mainly used for printing and patterns. It will only be activated if you have cut a line type. No fill means that you will not be printing anything. Print is one of the advantageous features that this machine offers because it allows you to print your designs and then cut them. It is what motivates a lot of people to get a Cricut in the first place because they love the look.

You have another option that says Select All. Moving objects can be very frustrating and cause you to become extremely irritated. Instead, click Select All. When you click Select All, you will be able to move them all at once.

The edit icon has a dropdown menu, and it gives you options to do the following:

- **Align:** Aligning will obviously tell you where you are going, and it will tell you if you are going to go left, right, and things of that nature.

- **Distribute:** Distributing is for spacing between the elements. This is very time-consuming, and it is not always right if you are doing it on your own. The distribute button is going to help you do this and make sure that it is right.

- **Arrange:** Arranging just means where you are going to be putting the elements on the canvas.

- **Flip:** Flipping is going to reflect your image.

- **Size:** Sizing is pretty self-explanatory. It just means modifying the size of your project.

- **Rotate:** Rotating means that you are turning your project on a specific angle.

- **Position:** Positioning means where you are putting your project.

- **Font:** The font option means which font you are using and what style of lettering you are doing.

- **Style:** The style of what you can have means bold, italics, and things of that nature.

- **Curve:** The curving means that you can curve your text.

- **Advance:** The advanced options allow you to ungroup letters and to group your letters as well as other options.

All of these have different options for what you can do with your projects, so it is a great idea to explore them and understand what they can do for you. This is why we have listed them for you.

Your left panel is for inserting shapes, images, and other items. This panel has seven options which means that you can create and replace new project templates. This means that you will have a guide on the type of things that you are going to be using for your projects. This is where you can add ready-to-cut projects from Access. You can see images, and this is where you can select images, text, shapes, and uploads. If you have Cricut Access, the images and ready-to-cut projects, and other options like fonts are available to you, and it will not cost you. However, if you do not have Cricut Access, they all cost money; you will have to pay for them. This adds up extremely quickly.

The right panel is all about layering. Layers represent every element or design on your canvas. So think of it like putting on your clothes when you get dressed. So, let us imagine that you live somewhere that is very cold. If you live somewhere that is cold, you are going to have an inner layer of underthings, but then you are also going to have pants, socks, a shirt, and the basics. You will also have a hat, gloves, boots, and other items to fight off the cold. The same will happen to your design depending on how complex your project is. You will have different types of layers that you need to make up your project on.

When you Group or ungroup, you are grouping layers or ungrouping layers, which is very simple. Delete just means that you are deleting any elements that you have decided that you do not want.

You have Layer Visibility and Line Type Fill which we have already gone over. Layer Visibility simply means that you are looking at the visibility of your design. The icon should look like a little eyeball. You will also have Wheel, Attach, Flatten, Contour, or Slice. These tools are especially important because they will let you change your project and take it to the next level. The Slicing tool is perfect for cutting out shapes or other elements from different designs. Attaching works like grouping the layers, but it is more powerful by offering the ability to remain in place. The Flatten option means that you are selecting the layers you want to print together as a whole, and then you can click Flatten. In this case, the element will become a print and then cut design.

Chapter 7.
Glossary of Common Vocabulary

When working with the Cricut cutting machines and Design Space, you are going to come across different terminology. The following is a glossary of the Cricut vocabulary to help you understand the system better. The following is the general terminology for both Cricut and Design Space.

Backing

The backing is the back sheet of material such as vinyl. It is the part of the material that gets stuck onto the cutting mat and is usually the last part of the material to be removed after cutting, weeding, and the project transfer.

Bleed

The bleed refers to a space around each item to be cut. This gives the cutting machine the ability to make a more precise cut. It is a small border that separates cutting items on a page. This option can be turned off, but it is not recommended.

Bonded Fabric

Bonded fabric is a material that is not very elastic. It is held together with adhesive and is not a typical woven type fabric.

If there is some gunk visible on the blade, pinch around the blade shaft using a very careful grip with your opposite thumb and forefinger, and bring it back, making sure you don't go against the blade angle as you do.

This will remove any foreign material from your blade tip and make your cuts more accurate. You may also take a ball of tin foil and poke the blade a few times into it, which will remove debris while also allowing a minor sharpening on them.

Blade

Cricut has a few different types of cutting blades and tips. Each blade has its own unique function enabling it to cut various materials.

Blade Housing

The blade housing is the cylindrical tube that holds the blade and fits into the blade head and blade accessory compartment of the Cricut cutting machine.

Blank

Cricut offers items, called blanks, to use with various projects for vinyl, iron-on, heat transfer vinyl, or infusible ink. These items include T-shirts, tote bags, coasters, and baby rattles.

Brayer

The Brayer is a tool that looks a bit like a lint roller brush. It is used to flatten and stick material or objects down smoothly as it irons out bubbles, creases, etc.

Bright Pad

A Bright Pad is a device that looks like a tablet. This device has a strong backlight to light up materials to help with weeding and defining intricate cuts. It is a very handy tool to have and can be used for other DIY projects as well.

Butcher Paper

Butcher paper is the white paper that comes with the Cricut Infusible Inks sheets. It is used to act as a barrier between the EasyPress or iron when transferring the ink sheet onto a blank or item.

Carriage

The carriage is the bar in the Cricut cutting machine which the blade moves across.

Cartridge

Cartridges are what the older models of the Cricut cutting machine used to cut images. Each cartridge would hold a set of images.

They can still be used with the Cricut Explore Air 2, which has a docking site for them.

If you want to use them with a Cricut Maker, you will have to buy the USB adaptor. Design Space still supports the use of Cartridge images. Cartridges also come in a digital format.

Cricut Maker Adaptive Tool System

The Cricut Maker comes with an advanced tools system control using intricate brass gears.

These new tools have been designed to aid the machine in making precise cuts and being able to cut more materials such as wood, metal, and leather.

Cut Lines

These are the lines along which the cutting machine will cut out the project's shapes.

Cutting Mat

There are a few different types of cutting mats, also known as machine mats. Most of the large mats can be used on both the Cricut Explore Air 2 and the Cricut Maker. The Cricut Joy needs mats that are designed specifically for it.

Cut Screen

When you are creating projects in Design Space, there is a green button on the top right-hand corner of the screen called the Make it button.

When the project is ready to be cut, this button is clicked on. Once that button has been clicked, the user is taken to another screen where they will see how the project is going to be cut out. This is the Cut Screen.

Drive Housing

The Drive Housing is different from the Blade Housing in that it has a gold wheel at the top of the blade. These blades can only be used with the Cricut Maker cutting machine.

EasyPress

A Cricut EasyPress is a handheld pressing iron that is used for iron-on, heat transfer vinyl (HTV), and infusible ink. EasyPress's latest models are the EasyPress 2 and the EasyPress Mini.

EasyPress Mat

There are a few different EasyPress Mat sizes that are available on the market. These mats make transferring iron-on, heat transfer vinyl, and infusible ink a lot simpler.

These mats should be used for these applications instead of an ironing board to ensure the project's success.

Firmware

Firmware is a software patch, update, or newly added functionality for a device. For cutting machines, it would be new driver's updates, cutting functionality, and so on.

Both Design Space software, Cricut cutting machines, and Cricut EasyPress 2 machines need to have their Firmware updated regularly.

Go Button

This can also be called the "Cut" button. This is the button on the Cricut cutting or EasyPress machine that has the green Cricut "C" on it. It is the button that is pressed when a project is ready to be cut or pressed for the EasyPress models.

JPG File

A JPG file is a common form of a digital image. These image files can be uploaded for use with a Design Space project.

Kiss Cut

When the cutting machine cuts through the material but not the material backing sheet, it is called a Kiss Cut.

Libraries

Libraries are lists of images, fonts, or projects that have been uploaded by the user or maintained by Cricut Design Space.

PNG File

A PNG file is another form of a graphics (image) file. It is most commonly used in Web-based graphics for line drawings, small graphic/icon images, and text.

Ready to Do Projects

Design Space contains ready-to-do projects, which are the ones that have already been designed. All the user has to do is choose the project to load in Design Space, get the material ready, and then make it to cut the design out. These projects can be customized as well.

Scraper Tool

The Scraper tool comes in small and large. It is used to make sure the material sticks firmly to a cutting mat, object, or transfer sheet.

Self-Healing Mat

Cricut has many handy accessories and tools to help with a person's crafting. One of these handy tools is the Self-Healing Mat.

This mat is not for use in a cutting machine but can be used with handheld slicing tools to cut material to exact specifications.

SVG File

The SVG file format is the most common format for graphic files in Cricut Design Space. This is because these files can be manipulated without losing their quality.

Transfer Sheet/Paper

A transfer sheet or transfer paper is a sheet that is usually clear and has a sticky side.

These sheets are used to transfer various materials like transfer vinyl, sticker sheets, and so on onto an item.

Weeding/Reverse Weeding

Weeding is the process of removing vinyl or material from a cut pattern or design that has been left behind after removing the excess material—for example, weeding the middle of the letter "O" to leave the middle of it hollow. Reverse Weeding would be leaving the middle of the letter "O" behind and removing the outside of it.

Weeding Tool

The Weeding tool has a small hooked head with a sharp point. This tool is used to pick off the material that is not needed on a cut. For instance, when cutting out the letter "O," the weeding tool is used to remove the middle of the letter so that it is hollow. Cleaning up a cut design with the Weeding tool is called weeding.

PART 4.

CRICUT PROJECT IDEAS

-

Chapter 1.
Paper Projects

Paper Flowers

Supplies Needed:

- "Cricut Maker" or "Cricut Explore"
- Cutting Mat
- Cardstock
- Adhesive

Instructions:

1. Log in to the Design Space application and click on the "New Project" button on the top right corner of the screen to view a blank canvas.
2. Click on the "Images" icon on the "Design Panel" and type in "flower" in the search bar. Go to "desired image," then click on the "Insert Images" button at the bottom of the screen.
3. The selected image will be displayed on the canvas and can be edited using applicable tools from the "Edit Image Bar."
4. The design is ready to be cut. Simply click on the "Make It" button, load the cardstock to your "Cricut" machine and follow the instructions on the screen to cut your project.
5. Once the design has been cut, simply remove the cut flowers and bend them at the center, then using the adhesive, stack the flowers with the largest flowers at the bottom.

Leafy Garland

Supplies Needed:

- Cardstock, 2 or more colors of green or white to paint yourself
- Glue gun
- LightGrip cutting mat
- Weeding tool or pick
- Floral wire
- Floral tape

Instructions:

1. Open Cricut Design Space and create a new project.
2. Select the "Image" button in the lower left-hand corner and search for "leaf collage."
3. Select the leaves image and click "Insert."
4. Place your cardstock on the cutting mat.
5. Send the design to your Cricut.
6. Remove the outer edge of the paper, leaving the leaves on the mat.
7. Use a pick or scoring tool to score down the center of each leaf lightly.
8. Use your weeding tool or carefully pick to remove the leaves from the mat.
9. Gently bend each leaf at the scoreline.
10. Glue the leaves into bunches of two or three.
11. Cut a length of floral wire to your desired garland size, and wrap the ends with floral tape.
12. Attach the leaf bunches to the wire using floral tape.
13. Continue attaching leaves until you have a garland of the size you want. Bundle lots of leaves for a really full look, or spread them out to be sparser.
14. Create hooks at the ends of the garland with floral wire.
15. Hang your beautiful leaf garland wherever you'd like!

DIY Bookmark Cat-page

Supplies Needed:

- Block of 20 multi-colored poster board sheets
- Glue
- Pouch of 24 decorated colored pencils
- 6 round movable eyes Ø 12mm
- Perfo Round Clamp 6MM
- 5m roll of Glitter masking tape, green
- 5m roll of Glitter masking tape, white

Instructions:

1. Print the template and choose its paper colors.
2. Cut out the template along the lines.
3. Copy the drawing of the body, front legs, and back legs on the brown sheet, do the same in the purple sheet for the belly, and cut out.
4. Glue the elements together with glue.
5. To facilitate the gluing, put a little glue on a cardboard plate and use a brush to spread the glue well. Then clean the brush with warm water and soap.
6. Glue the movable eyes, glue a piece of masking tape to make the collar, cut a piece of pink paper in a triangle for the nose, and with a black pencil, draw the mouth, mustaches, and legs.
7. With the hole punch, make a small circle in the yellow paper and glue it to finalize the cat's collar.
8. To get an easy triangle nose, first cut out a square and cut it in half diagonally.
9. Write your name on the cat's belly with a colored pencil.
10. And there you have a nice cat-page bookmark for your summer readings. I'm going to reread the adventures of the little wizard, and what will you read?
11. You can even do it in other colors so that it doesn't get boring!

Crepe Paper Bouquet

Supplies Needed:

- "Cricut Maker" or "Cricut Explore"
- Standard grip mat
- Crepe paper in desired colors
- Floral wire
- Floral tape
- Hot glue
- Fern fronds
- Vase

Instructions:

1. Log in to the Design Space application and click on the "New Project" button on the top right corner of the screen to view a blank canvas.
2. Let's use an already existing project from the "Cricut" library and customize it. So, click on the "Projects" icon and type in "crepe bouquet" in the search bar.
3. Click on "Customize" so you can further edit the project to your preference, or simply click on the "Make It" button, load the crepe paper to your "Cricut" machine and follow the instructions on the screen to cut your project.
4. To assemble the design, follow the assembly instructions provided under the "Assemble" section of the project details.

Leaf Banner

Supplies Needed:

- "Cricut Maker" or "Cricut Explore"
- Standard grip mat
- Watercolor paper and paint
- Felt balls
- Needle and thread
- Hot glue

Instructions:

1. Log in to the Design Space application and click on the "New Project" button on the top right corner of the screen to view a blank canvas.

2. Let's use an already existing project from the "Cricut" library and customize it. So, click on the "Projects" icon and type in "leaf banner" in the search bar.

3. Click on "Customize" so you can further edit the project to your or simply click on the "Make It" button, load the watercolor paper to your "Cricut" machine and follow the instructions on the screen to cut your project.

4. Use watercolors to paint the leaves and let them dry completely. Then create a garland using the needle and thread through the felt balls and sticking the leaves to the garland with hot glue.

Chapter 2:
Vinyl Projects

Easy Iron-on Vinyl T-shirt

Supplies Needed:

- Iron-on vinyl
- One cotton T-shirt
- Weeding tool
- Craft knife
- Iron, EasyPress, or something to help you press the vinyl on the T-shirt
- Free SVG cut files or your designs

Instructions:

1. Start your Cricut Design Space and click on the "New project" button. Next, you will access the "Templates" option on your left editing panel. You will notice a template for a "Classic T-shirt" design. Click on the "Classic T-shirt" icon to specify the size of the project, style, and color.

2. Once you have chosen specifications for your T-shirt template and selected the design you wish to use on the T-shirt. You can manipulate the size and proportions by clicking on the elements of the T-shirt design.

3. Before you start cutting, you will need to prepare the mat and switch the "Mirror" option on. Remember that elements need to be mirrored for all iron-on designs before cutting.

4. Before clicking on "Make it" to start cutting your design, you need to make sure that the iron-on vinyl is facing the mat with the shiny side of it pressed down to it. The next step will require some patience on your side—as well as some weeding action—so brace yourself for step number 5.

5. Now, when your iron-on vinyl design is ready, you can start weeding. You have already had a chance to learn what weeding is as well as everything about weeding tools—you will use your weeding tool of choice to remove all excess vinyl that you don't need in your design. Vinyl won't come off that easy, so you need to start peeling carefully from the edges. Start from the matte side of the design by peeling off vinyl from one edge with your tool. Make a small cut on the corner; then, you can peel the vinyl with your finger or by using the weeding tool. Don't cut through—just make a small cut so that you would be able to peel the vinyl off.

6. Now it's time to apply the iron-on vinyl design to your cotton T-shirt. You can use an iron or EasyPress Cricut iron, as specified under materials you need to use for this project. In case you are using EasyPress, you can find guidelines that should help you with ironing and applying the design to the T-shirt.

7. You can choose the type of press you are using, then specify your heat-transfer material and select the base material you are using. For this project, we have used everyday iron-on vinyl, and our base material is a 100% cotton T-shirt. Once you choose the preferences, you will click on "Apply," the green button found on the bottom of the EasyPress guide page to make your craft.

Personalized Phone Case

Supplies Needed:

- Foil Adhesive Vinyl
- Transfer tape
- Clear phone case, more room for fun!
- Weeding tool
- Scissors or scalpel
- Cricut machine, Cricut Maker, or Cricut Explore Air

Instructions:

1. As always, when starting out fresh, click on "New Project" to open a blank canvas. You can make this project a breeze by clicking on "Templates." Here you can find templates for numerous different projects, which include phone cases as well. Choose the phone case template. Make sure to size the template layer to fit the size of the clear phone case you have prepared for the project. From there, you can start working on your design. You can add images of your choice and resize them as needed to make a phone case design. Once your design is ready to go, you will click "Select All" then choose the "Attach" option. This will prepare the design for cutting as you need both the phone case recmat layer cut out and the designs used for the phone case.

2. If you are happy with your design, you can click on "Make it." Before proceeding with cutting, choose Foil Adhesive Vinyl as your material. Set up the cutting mat and prepare the material to start cutting.

3. Now that your design is cut out, it's time to use the weeding tool. Remove all excess vinyl from the design—in this case, and excess material would be the background while your designs (butterflies, for example) should remain intact. Next, attach the transfer tape to the vinyl and remove the backing paper. Attach the vinyl to the phone case with the transfer tape.

4. You will use your scissors or a scalpel to remove the excess part of the vinyl once it is attached to the phone case—remove those parts that don't fit the phone case design. For instance, you will need to remove the part of the vinyl piece covering the camera slot on the phone case. Remove the tape, and voila! You have your own personalized phone case. You can make as many designs as you like using these guidelines.

Personalized Pillow Case

- Materials
- Iron-on Vinyl
- Pillowcase
- Weeding tool
- Cricut Machine
- EasyPress or iron

Instructions:

1. Upload your preferred design or choose one from the "Design Space" image library. You can also make your own design. Make sure to adjust the size of the image to the size of the pillow— you don't want the image to be too small, but also, you don't want it to go over the entire surface of the pillow. You can also create a mock-up statement or a witty citation by using a font of your choice. When your design is ready, you can proceed to "Make it," there, you will specify iron-on vinyl as your material of choice. Make sure to use "Mirror" on your design as you will be attaching the image to the pillow. Before you start cutting the image with the machine, set up your cutting mat and arrange the material. Proceed to cut.

2. Your design is cut, and now it's the time for weeding. Take your weeding tool and start removing all the excess vinyl from your design until only the image you want on the pillow is left. Remove all vinyl scraps from the working surface and prepare your EasyPress or regular iron. Heat your EasyPress—you can set the timer on.

3. The heating up will take 5 seconds. Afterward, you will heat the pillow surface for 30 seconds before attaching the design to the pillow. Place the vinyl on the pillow where you want the image to be, then use the Press again. Make sure to apply mild pressure onto the Press and hold for 15 seconds.

4. Let the vinyl piece cool a bit before you remove it from the pillow and reveal your new design. At this moment, the vinyl is too hot, so you can burn your fingers. Once the vinyl piece is cool or warm, you can remove it and enjoy your design.

Vinyl Easter Eggs

Supplies Needed:

- The Cricut Explore machine
- Contact Papers
- The White Craft Eggs
- Vinyl (The Easter eggs are white, so I used black)

Instructions:

1. Get a free SVG, PNG, DXF file online, or you just create one yourself. Upload to the Cricut Design Space and gather your supplies. I got these Easter eggs for just $2.

2. Make some little tweaks to the design in the design space. You should remember that the design measurement should be very small to match the size of the egg. I made use of 1x1 inches for all the eggs. Then you weed out the cut images too.

3. Spread over your contact paper and adhere them to the eggs.

4. Peel off the contact paper to expose the egg.

5. Repeat the same process for the remaining eggs.

Vinyl Sticker Car Window

Supplies Needed:

- Cricut machine
- Premium outdoor glossy vinyl
- Transfer tape
- Scraper tool

Instructions:

1. Get and save the image you want to use online.
2. Log in to the Cricut design space and start a new project.
3. Click on the Upload icon and upload the saved image.
4. Click on the image and drag it to the next page, then select the image type.
5. Select the parts of the image you do not want as part of the final cut.
6. Select the image as a cut image. You will get the preview image as a cut image.
7. Approve the cut image. You would be redirected to the first upload screen.
8. Click on your just finished cut file, then highlight it and insert the image.
9. The image is added to your design space for size readjusting. The image is ready to cut.
10. Cut the image, and remove excessive vinyl after the image is cut.
11. Apply a layer of transfer tape to the top of the cut vinyl.
12. Clean the car window really well with rubbing alcohol to remove all dirt.
13. Carefully peel away the paperback of the vinyl.
14. Apply the cut vinyl on the window. Start at one end and roll it down.
15. Go over the applied vinyl with a scraper tool to remove the air bubble underneath the vinyl.
16. Slowly peel away the transfer tape from the window.

Perpetual Calendar

Supplies Needed:

- Unfinished woodblock calendar
- Acrylic paint in the color(s) of your choice
- Vinyl color(s) of your choosing
- Vinyl transfer tape
- Cutting mat
- Weeding tool or pick
- Mod Podge

Instructions:

1. Paint the woodblock calendar in the colors you'd like and set it aside to dry.
2. Open Cricut Design Space, and create a new project.
3. Create a square of the correct size for the four blocks.
4. Select the "Text" button in the lower left-hand corner.
5. Choose your favorite font and type the following numbers as well as all of the months: 0, 0, 1, 1, 2, 2, 3, 4, 5, 6, 7, 8.
6. Place your vinyl on the cutting mat.
7. Send the design to your Cricut.
8. Use a weeding tool or pick to remove the excess vinyl from the text.
9. Apply transfer tape to each separate number and the months.
10. Remove the paper backing from the tape and apply for the numbers as follows, 0 and 5 on the top and bottom of the first block. 1, 2, 3, 4 around the sides of the first block. 0 and 8 on the top and bottom of the second block. 1, 2, 6, 7 around the sides of the second block.
11. Remove the paper backing from the tape on the months, and apply them to the long blocks, the first six months on one and the second six months on the other.
12. Rub the tape to transfer the vinyl to the wood, making sure there are no bubbles.

13. Carefully peel the tape away. Seal everything with a coat of Mod Podge. Arrange your calendar to display today's date and enjoy it year after year!

Chapter 3.
Fabric Projects

Monogrammed Drawstring Bag

Supplies Needed:

- Two matching fabric recmats
- Needle and thread
- Ribbon
- Heat transfer vinyl
- Cricut EasyPress or iron
- Cutting mat
- Weeding tool or pick

Instructions:

1. Open Cricut Design Space and create a new project.
2. Select the "Image" button in the lower left-hand corner and search "monogram."
3. Select the monogram of your choice and click "Insert."
4. Place the iron-on material shiny liner side down on the cutting mat.
5. Send the design to the Cricut.
6. Use the weeding tool or pick to remove excess material.
7. Remove the monogram from the mat.
8. Center the monogram on your fabric, then move it a couple of inches down so that it won't be folded up when the ribbon is drawn. Iron the design onto the fabric.
9. Place the two recmats together, with the outer side of the fabric facing inward. Sew around the edges, leaving a seam allowance. Leave the top open and stop a couple of inches down from the top. Fold the top of the bag down until you reach your stitches.
10. Sew along the bottom of the folded edge, leaving the sides open.

11. Turn the bag right side out.
12. Thread the ribbon through the loop around the top of the bag.
13. Use your new drawstring bag to carry what you need!

Forever Fabric Banner

Supplies Needed:

- "Cricut Maker" or "Cricut Explore"
- Fabric grip mat
- Glitter iron-on (black, pink)
- "Cricut EasyPress"
- Weeder
- Pink ribbon
- Canvas fabric
- Sewable fabric stabilizer
- Sewing machine and thread

Instructions:

1. Log into the "Design Space" application and click on the "New Project" button on the top right corner of the screen to view a blank canvas.

2. Click on the "Projects" icon and type in "fabric banner" in the search bar.

3. Click on "Customize" to further edit the project to your preference, or simply click on the "Make It" button. Place the trimmed fabric on the cutting mat removing the paper backing, then load it to your "Cricut" machine and follow the instructions on the screen to cut your project. Similarly, load the iron-on vinyl sheet to the "Cricut" and cut the design, making sure to mirror the image.

4. Carefully remove the excess material from the sheet using the "weeder tool," making sure only the design remains on the clear liner.

5. Using the "Cricut EasyPress Mini" and "EasyPress Mat," the iron-on layers can be easily transferred to the fabric. Preheat your "EasyPress Mini," and put your iron-on vinyl design on the fabric and apply pressure for a couple of minutes or more. Wait for a few minutes before peeling off the design while it is still warm.

Fabric Flower Brooch

Supplies Needed:

- "Cricut Maker" or "Cricut Explore"
- Fabric grip mat
- Printable iron-on
- "Cricut EasyPress"
- Weeder, fabric
- Pencil pouch and inkjet printer

Instructions:

1. Log into the "Design Space" application and click on the "New Project" button on the top right corner of the screen to view a blank canvas.
2. Click on the "Projects" icon and type in "fabric pouch" in the search bar.
3. Click on "Customize" to further edit the project to your preference, or simply click on the "Make It" button and follow the prompts on the screen for using the inkjet printer to print the design on your printable vinyl and subsequently cut the design.
4. Carefully remove the excess material from the sheet using the "weeder tool," making sure only the design remains on the clear liner.
5. Using the "Cricut EasyPress Mini" and "EasyPress Mat," the iron-on layers can be easily transferred to the fabric. Preheat your "EasyPress Mini," and put your iron-on vinyl design on the fabric and apply pressure for a couple of minutes or more. Wait for a few minutes before peeling off the design while it is still warm.

Chapter 4.
Clothing projects

Print Socks

Supplies Needed:

- Socks
- Heat transfer vinyl
- Cutting mat
- Scrap cardboard
- Weeding tool or pick
- Cricut EasyPress or iron

Instructions:

1. Open Cricut Design Space and create a new project.
2. Select the "Image" button in the lower left-hand corner and search "paw prints."
3. Select the paw prints of your choice and click "Insert."
4. Place the iron-on material on the mat.
5. Send the design to the Cricut.
6. Use the weeding tool or pick to remove excess material.
7. Remove the material from the mat.
8. Fit the scrap cardboard inside of the socks.
9. Place the iron-on material on the bottom of the socks.
10. Use the EasyPress to adhere it to the iron-on material.
11. After cooling, remove the cardboard from the socks.
12. Wear your cute paw print socks!

DIY Baby Milestone Blanket

Supplies Needed:

- Cricut Machine
- Cricut EasyPress or Iron
- 2-3 sheets press on
- 1 1/4 yard white bandage texture
- Cricut Configuration Space document
- Autumn in November textual style

Instructions:

1. I cut out each number, and I've additionally incorporated the words month and months if you need to include that at the base. When using Cricut Press On, it's imperative to make sure to reflect the picture. You'll put the glossy side down on the mat and cut using the iron-on setting. Try not to use the HTV setting with your Creator. For unknown reasons, it is completely cut off. You simply need it to cut the vinyl and keep the transporter sheet unblemished.

2. Remove all the negative space, and after that, cut every month with the goal that you can space them on your cover. When using the Cricut EasyPress, you require a hard surface and an extended towel on that hard surface. You require something that will give a little with the goal that every one of the edges will be safely followed. You know you've got an awesome grip when you can see the surface of the material.

3. For Iron-On Lite, you'll require a temperature of 305°F and afterward press for 25-30 seconds. Give your things a decent warm-up in advance and after you're finished squeezing, turn your material over and press again for a couple of more seconds.

4. Now you're finished. So super simple, yet it requires a tad of investment to get your numbers equitably dispersed and to complete the edges of your material. You'll never need to spend $40+ on a Milestone infant cover again.

5. These DIY infant breakthrough covers are the best child shower blessings you can give. They're far superior, knowing you put your diligent work into something so unique.

Leather Flower Hat

Supplies Needed:

- "Cricut Maker" or "Cricut Explore," standard grip mat, Cricut Faux Leather, button, strong adhesive, and hat.

Instructions:

1. Log into the "Design Space" application and click on the "New Project" button on the top right corner of the screen to view a blank canvas.

2. Click on the "Projects" icon and type in "leather flower hat" in the search bar.

3. Click on "Customize" to further edit the project to your preference, or simply click on the "Make It" button and load the faux leather to your "Cricut" machine by placing it face down on the mat and follow the instructions on the screen to cut your project.

4. For assembly, glue tabs on each flower together to give shape to every single layer and let dry.

5. Glue all the flower layers on top of one another, with the biggest layer at the bottom; once the flower dries completely, glue a button on the center of the flower. And finally, glue the flower to the hat.

Chapter 5.
Glass Projects

Holiday Mirror Decoration

Supplies Needed:

- "Cricut Maker" or "Cricut Explore"
- Cutting mat
- Vinyl
- Transfer tape
- Scrapper

Instructions:

1. Log into the "Design Space" application and click on the "New Project" button on the top right corner of the screen to view a blank canvas.

2. Click on the "Images" icon and type in "reindeer" in the search bar. Select a picture that you like and click on "Insert Image."

3. Now type in "wreath" in the search bar and scroll down to find the image used in this project. Click on it, and a small icon will be added to the "Insert Image" bar at the bottom of the screen. Click on "Insert Images" at the bottom of the screen.

4. Edit the design and click on the "Fill" icon from the "Edit Bar" at the top of the screen to select "Print" and then change the color of the deer to red. Click on the lock icon at the bottom left of the deer image to adjust the image inside the wreath.

5. Select the entire design and click on the "Group" icon under the "Layers panel." Then click on "Save" to save the project.

6. The design is ready to be cut. Simply click on the "Make It" button and load the vinyl sheet to your "Cricut" machine and follow the instructions on the screen to cut the design.

7. Carefully remove the excess vinyl from the sheet and put the transfer tape on top of the cut design. After you have cleaned the mirror, slowly peel the paper backing on the vinyl from one end to the other in a rolling motion to ensure even placement. Now, use the scraper tool on top of the transfer tape to remove any bubbles, and then just peel off the transfer tape.

Wine Glass Decoration

Supplies Needed:

- "Cricut Maker" or "Cricut Explore"
- Cutting mat
- Vinyl (gold)
- Transfer tape
- Scrapper
- Wine glasses

Instructions:

1. Log into the "Design Space" application and click on the "New Project" button on the top right corner of the screen to view a blank canvas.
2. Let's use text for this project. Click on "Text" from the "Designs Panel" on the left of the screen and type in "WINE O'clock" or any other phrase you may like.
3. For the image below, the font "Anna's Fancy Lettering– Hannah" in purple was selected. But you can let your creativity take over this step and choose any color or font that you like. Select and copy-paste your image for the number of times you want to print your design.
4. Click on "Save" to save the project, then click on the "Make It" button and load the vinyl sheet to your "Cricut" machine and follow the instructions on the screen to cut the design.
5. Carefully remove the excess vinyl from the sheet. To easily paste your design on the wine glass without stretching the pieces, put the transfer tape on top of the cut design. After you have cleaned the surface, slowly peel the paper backing on the vinyl from one end to the other in a rolling motion to ensure even placement. Now, use the scraper tool on top of the transfer tape to remove any bubbles, and then just peel off the transfer tape.

Window Clings

Supplies Needed:

- Window cling
- Cricut machine
- Weeding tool
- Scrapper tool

Instructions:

1. Log in to the Cricut design space.
2. Create a new project.
3. Click on Upload Image.
4. Drag the image to the design space.
5. Highlight the image and "flatten" it.
6. Use the Make It button.
7. Place the window clings to the cutting mat.
8. Custom dial the machine to window cling.
9. Load the cutting mat into the machine.
10. Push the mat up against the rollers.
11. Cut the design out of the window cling.
12. Weed out the excess window cling.
13. Apply the cut design to the window.
14. Smoothen with a scraper tool to let out all air bubbles.

Live Love Laugh Glass Block

Supplies Needed:

- Glass block
- Frost spray paint
- Clear enamel spray
- Holographic vinyl
- Vinyl transfer tape
- Cutting mat
- Weeding tool or pick
- Fairy lights

Instructions:

1. Spray the entire glass block with frost spray paint, and let it dry.
2. Spray the glass block with a coat of clear enamel spray, and let it dry.
3. Open Cricut Design Space and create a new project.
4. Select the "Text" button in the Design Panel.
5. Type "Live Love Laugh" in the text box
6. Use the dropdown box to select your favorite font.
7. Arrange the words to sit on top of each other.
8. Place your vinyl on the cutting mat.
9. Send the design to your Cricut.
10. Use a weeding tool or pick to remove the excess vinyl from the design.
11. Apply transfer tape to the design.
12. Remove the paper backing and apply the words to the glass block.
13. Smooth down the design and carefully remove the transfer tape.
14. Place fairy lights in the opening of the block, leaving the battery pack on the outside.
15. Enjoy your decorative quote!

Unicorn Wine Glass

Supplies Needed:

- Stemless wine glasses
- Vinyl transfer tape
- Cutting mat
- Weeding tool or pick
- Extra fine glitter in the color of your choice
- Mod Podge

Instructions:

1. Open Cricut Design Space and create a new project.
2. Select the "Text" button in the Design Panel.
3. Type "It's not drinking alone if my unicorn is here."
4. Using the dropdown box, select your favorite font.
5. Adjust the positioning of the letters, rotating some to give a whimsical look.
6. Select the "Image" button on the Design Panel and search for "unicorn."
7. Select your favorite unicorn and click "Insert," then arrange your design how you want it on the glass.
8. Place your vinyl on the cutting mat, making sure it is smooth and making full contact.
9. Send the design to your Cricut.
10. Use a weeding tool or pick to remove the excess vinyl from the design. Use the Cricut Bright Pad to help if you have one.
11. Apply transfer tape to the design, pressing firmly and making sure there are no bubbles.
12. Remove the paper backing and apply the words to the glass where you'd like them. Leave at least a couple of inches at the bottom for the glitter.
13. Smooth down the design and carefully remove the transfer tape.
14. Coat the bottom of the glass in Mod Podge, wherever you would like glitter to be. Give the area a wavy edge.

15. Sprinkle glitter over the Mod Podge, quickly working before it dries.
16. Add another layer of Mod Podge and glitter, and set it aside to dry.
17. Cover the glitter in a thick coat of Mod Podge.
18. Allow the glass to cure for at least 48 hours.
19. Enjoy drinking from your unicorn wine glass!

Window Decoration

Supplies Needed:

- "Cricut Maker" or "Cricut Explore"
- Cutting mat
- Orange window cling (non-adhesive material that has static cling so it can be easily applied on the glass; since it does not have sticky cling like vinyl, make sure you put this on the inner side of the window to protect exposure from external weather).

Instructions:

1. To start a new project, after you have logged into your "Cricut" account on "Design Space," click on the "New Project" button on the top right corner of the screen, and a blank canvas will be displayed.

2. Let's use an already existing project from the "Cricut" library and customize it. So click on the "Projects" icon on the "Design Panel" and click on the "All Categories" dropdown menu to view all existing projects that you can select from. For this example, we will click on "Home Decor" then type in "window" in the search bar to narrow your search to window cling projects.

3. You can view all the projects available by clicking on them, and a pop-up window displaying all the details of the project will appear on your screen.

4. The project selected for this example is displayed in the picture below. Click "Customize" at the bottom of the screen so you can edit the design as desired.

5. Your selected design will be displayed on the Canvas. You can see in the "Layers Panel" that this design contains multiple layers, but the two bottom layers are hidden from the canvas and will be excluded from being cut.

6. The design is ready to be printed and cut. Simply click on the "Make It" button on the top right corner of the screen. You will see the required mats and material displayed on the screen.

7. Load the orange window cling to your "Cricut" machine and click "Continue" at the bottom right corner of the screen to start cutting your design.

8. As a note, the "Continue" button will not appear if you used images and/or fonts for your design that are not free and available for purchase only. You will instead see a "Purchase" at the bottom right of the screen, so you can buy the image or font first, and once the purchase has been made, the "Continue" button will be available to you.

9. Once your "Cricut" device has been connected to your computer, set your cut setting to "Vinyl." It is recommended to use this setting to cut the sticker paper since it tends to be thicker than regular paper. Place the sticker paper on top of the cutting mat and load it into the "Cricut" device by pushing against the rollers. The "Load/Unload" button will start flashing, so just press it. Then press the "Go" button, which would already be flashing. Voila! You have window decorations ready for Halloween.

Chapter 6.
Business Projects

Easter Basket Fun

Supplies Needed:

- Pink Cricut cardstock
- Blue Cricut cardstock
- Pink Cricut glitter tape
- Clear Cricut sticker paper
- Green Standard Grip mat
- Cricut Fine-Point Blade
- Stylus scoring pen or wheel
- Weeding tool
- Scraping tool or brayer tool
- Pair of scissors for cutting the material to size
- Inkjet printer
- Glue dots or hot glue gun

Instructions:

1. Open a new project in Design Space.
2. Select "Pentagon" from the "Shapes" menu on the left-hand side.
3. Change the background color to blue.
4. Leave the shape as the default size.
5. Select "Square" from the "Shapes" menu on the left-hand side.
6. Leave the background color as the default color.
7. Unlock the shape and change it to 3.375" wide and 3.139" long.
8. Move the pentagon to the following position on the screen: x = 1.986 and y = 1.833.

9. Move the square over the top point of the pentagon in the following position on the screen: x = 1.972 and y = 0.

10. Select the square and the pentagon. To not disturb the slice, select the objects from the "Layers" panel on the right-hand side of the screen.

11. Select the 2 objects by first selecting the square, holding down the "Ctrl" key on the keyboard, then selecting the pentagon.

12. Right-click and select "Slice."

13. Remove all the slices and delete them.

14. Remove the 2 triangle objects but do not delete them; instead, move them out of the way.

15. Change the sliced pentagon to the following size: width = 5.75" and height = 2.724".

16. Select "Square" from the "Shapes" menu on the left-hand side.

17. Change the background color to blue.

18. Unlock the shape and change it to 3.111 wide and 2.724 long.

19. Create a duplicate of the square.

20. Unlock the duplicate square and change it to 4.724 wide and 4.724 long.

21. Move the larger square to the following position on the screen: x = 4.306 and y = 3.361.

22. Move the pentagon to the following position on the screen: x = 2.955 and y = 0.611.

23. Move the smaller square to the following position on the screen: x = 5.917 and y = 0.611.

24. Select the pentagon shape and the smaller square shape, right-click, and select "Weld." This is the box's side.

25. Select "Score Line" from the "Shapes" menu on the left-hand side.

26. Unlock the shape and change the height to 2.724".

27. Move the score line to the following position on the screen: x = 4.333 and y = 0.847.

28. Create a duplicate of the score line and move over to the side.

29. Swivel the score line, so it runs horizontally.

30. Unlock the shape and change it to 3.111" width.
31. Move the score line to the following position on the screen: x = 4.306 and y = 3.361.
32. Select the box side and the 2 score lines, right-click, and select "Attach."
33. Create 3 duplicates of the box side with score lines.
34. Rotate each of the box sides and fit them together around the square.
35. When all the sides are attached to the square, it will resemble a flattened box.
36. Select "Square" from the "Shapes" menu on the left-hand side.
37. Change the background color to pink.
38. Unlock the shape and change it to 3.111" width and 2.724" length.
39. Select "Images" from the menu on the left-hand side.
40. Change the background color to pink.
41. Find an image of bunny ears. This project uses #M8620AE4 as an example.
42. Unlock the shape and change it to 1.276" wide and 1.168" long.
43. Create a duplicate of the bunny ears.
44. Move the bunny ears over the top of the pink square.
45. Flip the duplicate of the bunny ears vertically and attach the image to the bottom of the pink recmat.
46. Select the pink square and both bunny ear images, right-click, and select 'Attach.'
47. Select 'Score Line' from the 'Shapes' menu on the left-hand side.
48. Unlock the shape and change the height to 0.847".
49. Swivel the score line so it runs horizontally.
50. Create a duplicate of the score line and move it over to the side.
51. Move the one score line to just below the bunny ears on the top of the pink recmat. It must fit perfectly into the pink square.
52. Do the same for the second score line at the bottom of the pink recmat.

53. Select the pink recmat and the score lines, right-click, and select 'Attach.'
54. Save the project.
55. Make sure the scoring stylus is loaded into the Cricut.
56. Set the Cricut dial to cardstock.
57. In Design Space, click 'Make it.'
58. Position the box on the mat so it fits with enough bleed around the edges of the cutting board.
59. Make sure the bunny handle is not flush against the side of the pink cutting board.
60. Load the appropriate color material, which is going to be blue cardstock for the basket and pink cardstock for the bunny handle.
61. When the basket and handle have printed, use the glue dots to glue the basket sides together.
62. Where each side of the box folds into the other, you will need to make a small snip at the bottom to free the fold.
63. When the basket is assembled, stick the pink Cricut glitter ribbon around it.
64. Fold the bunny ears on the bottom of the handle up against the recmat and glue them into position.
65. Where the bunny ears fold up onto the handle will be where you will stick the hand onto the basket.
66. Fill with Easter goodies.

Wooden Gift Tags

Supplies Needed:

- Balsa wood
- Gold vinyl
- Vinyl transfer tape
- Cutting mat
- Weeding tool or pick

Instructions:

1. Secure your small balsa wood pieces to the cutting mat, then tape the edges with masking tape for additional strength.
2. Open Cricut Design Space and create a new project.
3. Select the shape you would like for your tags and set the Cricut to cut wood, then send the design to the Cricut.
4. Remove your wood tags from the Cricut and remove any excess wood.
5. In Cricut Design Space, select the "Text" button in the lower left-hand corner.
6. Choose your favorite font, and type the names you want to place on your gift tags.
7. Place your vinyl on the cutting mat.
8. Send the design to your Cricut.
9. Use a weeding tool or pick to remove the excess vinyl from the text.
10. Apply transfer tape to the quote.
11. Remove the paper backing from the tape.
12. Place the names on the wood tags.
13. Rub the tape to transfer the vinyl to the wood, making sure there are no bubbles. Carefully peel the tape away.
14. Thread twine or string through the holes, and decorate your gifts!

Snowy Wreath

Supplies Needed:

- Grapevine wreath
- Silver berry stems
- Spray adhesive
- Silver and white glitter
- Piece of wood to fit across the center of the wreath
- Wood stain, if desired
- Drill and a small bit
- Twine
- White vinyl
- Vinyl transfer tape
- Cutting mat
- Weeding tool or pick

Instructions:

1. Thread the silver berry stems throughout the grapevine wreath.
2. Use the spray adhesive and glitter to create patches of "snow" on the wreath.
3. If you want to stain your wood, do so now and set it aside to dry. Open Cricut Design Space and create a new project.
4. Select the "Text" button in the lower left-hand corner.
5. Choose your favorite font and type, "Let it snow."
6. Place your vinyl on the cutting mat.
7. Send the design to your Cricut.
8. Use a weeding tool or pick to remove the excess vinyl from the text. Apply transfer tape to the words.
9. Remove the paper backing and apply the design to the wood piece. Rub the tape to transfer the vinyl to the wood, making sure there are no bubbles. Carefully peel the tape away.
10. Drill two small holes in the corner of the wood and thread the twine through.
11. Hang your wreath and sign for the winter season!

Oogie Boogie Treat Packs

Supplies Needed:

- Burlap Support Packs
- Black Warmth Exchange (Press On) Vinyl
- Treats/Treats
- Cricut Producer or Investigate Air
- Heat Press or Iron

Instructions:

1. Open Oogie Boogie record in Configuration Space (this is an awesome instructional exercise that demonstrates well-ordered industry standards to transfer pictures in configuration space).
2. Change the extent of your Oogie Boogie face to accommodate your packs (I made mine 2" tall).
3. Duplicate outlines until the point when you have the same number of appearances as you do packs.
4. Load warmth exchange vinyl gleaming side down on light grasp slicing mat and send to cut.
5. Weed overabundance vinyl from around appearances and separate faces (the fundamental toolbox proves to be useful with this).
6. Preheat burlap sacks before squeezing (either with an iron or warmth press for no less than 5 seconds).
7. I found through experimentation that you have to push down longer on burlap to get the vinyl to stick. I've discovered that squeezing at 275° for 45 seconds gets everything squeezed splendidly.
8. Slowly peel plastic support from the left corner.
9. Fill your treat packs with fun treats.

Trick or Treat Bag (Easy)

Supplies Needed:

- "Cricut Maker" or "Cricut Explorer", standard grip mat, transfer tape, scraper, everyday vinyl, small craft paper bags.

Instructions:

1. To start a new project, after you have logged into your "Cricut" account on "Design Space", click on the "New Project" button on the top right corner of the screen and a blank canvas will be displayed.

2. Click on the "Images" icon on the "Design Panel" and type in "Halloween" in the search bar to use an image from the "Cricut Image Library" for this project and click on "Insert Images" at the bottom of the screen. The image selected is shown in the picture below.

3. Your selected images will appear on the Canvas and you can notice from the "Layers Panel" on the right that one of the images has multiple layers, which can be edited individually. You can edit either or both the image as needed, for example, you could resize the image based on the size of your craft bag and change the color or fill in a pattern in the image by selecting the image and clicking on the applicable tool on the "Edit Bar", as shown in the picture below.

4. Select the entire design and click on the "Group" icon on the top right of the screen under "Layers panel". Click on "Save" at the top right corner of the screen and enter a name for your project, for example, "trick or treat bag" and click "Save".

5. Now, your design is ready to be cut (you would need to print the design first if you selected a fill color or pattern). Simply click on the "Make It" button on the top right corner of the screen. You will see the required mats and material displayed on the screen.

6. Click "Continue" at the bottom right corner of the screen. After you have loaded the vinyl to the "Cricut" machine and print the design onto the paper.

7. Note – The "Continue" button will not appear if you used images and/or fonts for your design that are not free and available for purchase only. You will instead see a "Purchase" at the bottom right of the screen, so you can buy the image or font first and once the purchase has been made, the "Continue" button will be available to you.

8. Once your "Cricut" device has been connected to your computer, set your cut setting to "Vinyl". Place the vinyl on top of the cutting mat and load it into the "Cricut" machine by pushing against the rollers. The "Load/Unload" button will start flashing so just press it. Then press the "Go" button which would already be flashing.

9. Carefully remove the excess vinyl from the sheet. To easily paste your design on the craft bag without stretching the pieces, put the transfer tape on top of the cut design. Now, slowly peel the paper backing on the vinyl from one end to the other in a rolling motion to ensure even placement and use the scraper tool on top of the transfer tape to remove any bubbles, and then just peel off the transfer tape. Viola! You have your own customized Halloween trick or treat bags that may look like the picture below.

Cake Topper (Cake)

Supplies Needed:

"Cricut Maker" or "Cricut Explorer", standard grip mat, hot glue gun, bamboo skewer or wooden dowel, cardstock in desired colors (green, yellow, white).

Instructions:

- To start a new project, after you have logged into your "Cricut" account on "Design Space", click on the "New Project" button on the top right corner of the screen and a blank canvas will be displayed.

- Let's use text for this project. Click on "Text" from the "Designs Panel" on the left of the screen and type in "Oh" then click on the "Text" button again and type "BOY".

- Then align the two texts and click on the "Group" icon on the "Layers Panel". For the image below, the font "Close to My Heart - Artbooking" in Regular and color as shown in the picture below were selected. But you can let your creativity take over this step and choose any color or font that you like.

- Click on "Save" at the top right corner of the screen and give the desired name to the project, for example, "Cake Topper – Oh BOY" and click "Save".

- Your design is ready to be cut now. Simply click on the "Make It" button on the top right corner of the screen. You will see the required mats and material displayed on the screen. Load the material with printed design to your "Cricut" machine and click "Continue" at the bottom right corner of the screen to start cutting your design.

- Note – The font used is available for purchase so click on "Purchase" at the bottom right of the screen to buy the images before you can print them. And once you have made the purchase the "Continue" button will be available to you.

- Once your "Cricut" device has been connected to your computer, set your cut setting to cut your chosen material. Place the cardstock on top of the cutting mat and load it into the "Cricut" machine by pushing against the rollers. The "Load/Unload" button will start flashing so just press it. Then press the "Go" button which would already be flashing.
- Now use the hot glue gun to adhere the design onto a bamboo skewer or wooden dowel and Viola! You have your own customized cake topper that may look like the picture below.

244

Felt Roses

Supplies Needed:
- SVG files with 3D flower design
- Felt Sheets
- Fabric Grip Mat
- Glue Gun

Instructions:
1. First of all, upload your Flower SVG Graphics into the Cricut design space as explained in the "Tips" section ("How to import images into Cricut Design Space").
2. Having placed the image in the project, select it, right-click and click "Ungroup." This allows you to resize each flower independently of the others. Since you are using felt, it is recommended that each of the flowers is at least 6 inches in size.
3. Create several copies of the flowers, as many as you wish, selecting the colors you want in the Color Sync Panel (by dragging and dropping the images onto the color you would want them to be cut on). Immediately you're through with that, click on "Make it" on the Cricut design space.
4. Click on "Continue." After your Cricut Maker is connected and registered, under the "materials" options, select "Felt."
5. If your rotary blade is not in the machine, insert it. Next, on the Fabric Grip Mat, place the first felt sheet (in order of color), then, load them into your Cricut Maker. Press the "cut" button when this is done.
6. After they are cut, begin to roll the cut flowers one by one. Do this from the outside in. Make sure that you do not roll them too tight. Use the picture as a guide.
7. Apply Hot Glue on the circle right in the middle and press the felt flowers that you rolled up on the glue. Hold this in place and do not let it go until the glue binds it.
8. Wait for the glue to dry, and your roses are ready for use.

Hand Lettered Cake Topper

Supplies Needed:

- Glitter Card Stock
- Gold Paper Straw
- Cutting Mat
- Hot Glue Gun

Instructions:

1. Create your design in Cricut Design Space, or download your desired design and import it into Cricut Design Space using the instructions in the "Tips" section.
2. Resize the design as required.
3. Click the "Make it" button.
4. Select Glitter card stock as your material in Design Space and set the dial on your Cricut machine to "Custom."
5. Place the glitter card stock on your Cutting Mat and load it into the Cricut machine.
6. When this is done, press the "Cut" button on your Cricut machine.
7. After the machine is done with cutting the design, remove it from the mat. This can be done much more quickly using the Cricut Spatula tool.
8. Finally, using hot glue, stick cut-out design to the Gold Paper Straw and stick it in the cake as shown in the picture.

Recipe Stickers

Supplies Needed:

- "Cricut Maker" or "Cricut Explore", sticker paper, and cutting mat.

Instructions:

1. Log into the "Design Space" application and click on the "New Project" button on the top right corner of the screen to view a blank canvas.
2. Click on the "Images" icon on the "Design Panel" and type in "stickers" in the search bar. Click on the desired image, then click on the "Insert Images" button at the bottom of the screen.
3. The selected image will be displayed on the canvas and can be edited using applicable tools from the "Edit Image Bar". You can make multiple changes to the image as you need, for example, you could change the color of the image or change its size (sticker should be between 2-4 inches wide). The image selected for this project has the words "stickers" inside the design, so let's delete that by first clicking on the "Ungroup" button and selecting the "Stickers" layer, and clicking on the red "x" button. Click on the "Text" button and type in the name of your recipe, as shown in the picture below.
4. Drag and drop the text in the middle of the design and select the entire design. Now, click on "Align" and select "Center Horizontally" and "Center Vertically".
5. Select the entire design and click on the "Group" icon on the top right of the screen under "Layers panel". Now, copy and paste the designs and update the text for all your recipes.
6. Tip - Use your keyboard shortcut "Ctrl + C" and "Ctrl + V" to copy and paste the design.
7. Click on "Save" at the top right corner of the screen to name and save your project.
8. To cut your design, just click on the "Make It" button on the top right corner of the screen. Load the sticker paper to your

"Cricut" machine and click "Continue" at the bottom right corner of the screen to start cutting your design.

9. Note – The "Continue" button will only appear after you have purchased images and fonts that are available for purchase only.

10. Set your cut setting to "Vinyl" (recommended for sticker paper since it tends to be thicker than regular paper). Place the sticker paper on top of the cutting mat and follow the prompts on the screen to finish cutting your design. Viola! You have your own customized recipe stickers.

Custom Pads

Supplies Needed:

- "Cricut Maker" or "Cricut Explore", cutting mat and washi sheets or your choice of decorative paper/ crepe paper/ fabric.

Instructions:

1. Log into the "Design Space" application and click on the "New Project" button on the top right corner of the screen to view a blank canvas.

2. Using an already existing project from the "Cricut" library and customize it. So click on the "Projects" icon on the "Design Panel" and type in "pad" in the search bar.

3. Click on "Customize" so you can further edit the project to your preference. For example, the "unicorn pad" project shown below. You can click on the "Linetype Swatch" to change the color of the design.

4. The design is ready to be cut. Simply click on the "Make It" button and load the washi paper sheet to your "Cricut" machine and follow the instructions on the screen to cut your project.

Chapter 7.
Bonus

Halloween Party Stylistic Layout/Halloween Banner

Supplies Needed:

- Cricut Maker Machine
- Cricut Glitter Iron-On in S Fluorescent Orange, Silver, and Purple
- Wooden Skulls
- Felt Sheets
- Dark Rolled Jewels
- Arachnid Charms (comparable ones can be found at OTC)
- Arranged Sequins
- Grosgrain Ribbon
- Googly Eyes
- Felt Glue
- Craft glue Gun and Glue Sticks

Instructions:

1. To start, the Cricut Maker machine is used to remove flag pieces felt–two sheets every one of dark, orange, and purple felt brought about four pennant pieces for! each shading. After they are cut into the felt flag pieces, the Cricut Maker is utilized to remove the standard's structure components. The Maker's revolving cutting-edge slice through felt like margarine, and it worked like a fantasy! The two striped standard pieces are basically made with dark moved gems–simply slice to measure and paste

Mason Jars - Treat Bags

Supplies Needed:

- 5 9" by 12" Sheets of Black Glitter Craft Foam
- Pieces of Ribbon, little blossoms, or fall things to design the caps
- Heated glue firearm and paste sticks
- Cricut Explore Air 2 or Cricut Maker
- Access to Design Space
- Solid Grip Mat

Instructions:

1. Cut out the Items required You will require an aggregate of 3 cap tops, 3 edges subterranean insect the letters that spell BOO. Download the Halloween Mason Jars SVG and burden it into configuration space. It will load to scale (DO NOT meddle with the estimating or your caps won't fit!). Spot froth on the solid grasp mat and cut out the things.

Make the caps:

1. Since we're utilizing create froth there is no cover structured into the cone. Just take as much time as necessary and paste the crease together. Beginning at the base. Include heated glue an inch at once. When the cone is caused a slide it to up into the edge to ensure it fits.
2. At that point Glue on the edge from the underside of the cone. Presently include lace, roses, leaves, and whatever you like to the caps!
3. Bring everything together At that point community the letter on each container and heated glue it on. Fill the Halloween Mason Jars with treats. Spot the caps on the containers to finish the look! Rehash with the other two containers.

Unicorn Free Printable

Supplies Needed:

- Printable
- White Card Stock
- Cricut Mat
- Crepe Paper Streamers (varied colors)
- Gold Straws
- Glue Stick
- Hot Glue Gun
- Scissors

Instructions:

1. Import the printable image into Cricut Design Space.
2. Resize the PNG image and make it 5" wide.
3. With your Cricut machine, cut the unicorn head using the white cardstock. Also, print and cut out the "stickers."
4. After cutting out the pieces, stick the horn and the other elements using the glue stick.
5. In each color, cut out strips of crepe paper, about 2" wide; then, cut each strip into thirds.
6. On the reverse side of the unicorn head, glue the strips on the back edge (of the head), then glue them on the top by the horn. Ensure that only half the length of each strip is on this side, as you are going to glue the other half on the other side of the unicorn head.
7. Turn the unicorn head back over and glue the crepe streamers in place.
8. Turn the head over yet again and use hot glue to stick the gold paper straw onto the unicorn head reverse side to use as party props.

Valentine's Pillow

Supplies Needed:

- Cricut explore or maker machine
- Cricut 12" x 12" standard grip mat
- Cricut Weeder tool
- Purple iron-on
- Gold iron-on
- 20" x 20" pillow shape and protect
- EasyPress or iron
- Press fabric or clean cotton fabric

Instructions:

1. Download your favorite fonts. The fonts you will need to make this job are: Mastoc, Breamcatcher, and authentic Hilton. You have to download and install these fonts on the job to get the job done. To install, start the downloaded font (tagged.ttf) and put it in it on your pc. It works better if you download the fonts before launching the Cricut design space. Otherwise, you will want to close the browser and then reopen it after installing the fonts to automatically refresh your font record.

2. Produce design. Insert text on your canvas. The fonts will be automatically a part of this system fonts as soon as you've installed them. You can filter fonts in the design space by clicking system fonts from the top window. Once I have determined which words I need in each font, then I begin placing them at a design. The very first step would be to weld the script fonts collectively. Choose the words and ungroup the letters. Transfer the letters next to each other before you are happy with how they look. Then pick each of the letters and weld them together.

3. Organize all the words on your layout, pick all the words, and weld them together so that the words will reduce as one whole design.

4. Cut out design. In Cricut design space, cut pictures from iron-on. Make sure to check the "mirror pictures (for iron-on) "box at the mat preview before you cut (if cutting numerous mats, make certain to check that box to get every mat that has iron-on).

Valentine's Gift Tags

Supplies Needed:

- Cricut Machine Design Space
- Account Variety of card inventory
- Gold pen
- Cut designs you need to create this I Love You gift tag with your Cricut

Instructions:

1. Follow on-screen instructions to draw and cut each layer as required.
2. Glue the two layers of paper together, aligning the heart-shaped hole atop the tag.
3. Add the vinyl and burn to guarantee it adheres carefully. I can't apply vinyl, particularly glitter vinyl. You can attempt using the transfer tape, but the glitter tends not to stick to the transfer tape.
4. Add twine or ribbon to the tag and attach the tag as you like. You can use the tag back to write a unique signal to someone.
5. Alternatively, instead of using glue, you can bind the two cutouts together. Add these Valentine tags in your charms, embellishments, and fun accents.
6. Draw a beautiful accent design with your gold glitter pen. Add glitter vinyl word art to your Valentine tag
7. You can use this pleasant Valentine's Day Cricut project to produce all kinds of custom tags or use parts to make other types of projects. Change colors, materials, and wording.

Halloween Koozie

Supplies Needed:

- Cricut Maker
- Cricut EasyPress
- Can koozies
- Sparkle Iron-on
- Ordinary Iron-on
- Foil Iron-on
- Cricut Bright Pad
- Weeder instrument

Instructions:

1. Open the cut file for koozies in Cricut Design. Select the designs and the hues you might want for the layers of the structure for your Halloween koozies. At the point when prepared to cut, try to reflect the picture since we're pressing on. Cut.

2. Get rid of negative space from the structure. The Bright Pad makes this procedure MUCH simpler (especially because it tends to be difficult to see the cut lines on sparkle iron-on). Mastermind plan on the koozie to choose an arrangement.

3. Turn on EasyPress and set it to the temperature as shown on the reference sheet manual. Set the clock to the suggested time on the reference sheet.

4. Spread with a press material or material paper and hit the green Cricut catch to begin the clock and you start to push down with firm weight onto the Koozie.

5. Permit to cool for 2–3 minutes before endeavoring to strip back covering. On the off chance that the iron-on lifts with the coating don't evacuate it. Press it for 10 additional seconds and have a go at stripping back once more. If important, rehash until the liner lifts effectively leaving the structure on the koozie. The magnificence of the EasyPress is that this experimentation game is wiped out.

6. You know precisely what temperature to utilize and to what extent to press so there was no including additional time and seeking after the best. The EasyPress likewise has totally in any event, warming so there are no "problem areas" like a garments iron has.

7. Position the second layer of the structure (if relevant) and rehash the procedure above.

Conclusion

Now that you have completed this handy manual on how to use the Cricut machine, you should be well-equipped to head out into the Cricut crafting world and start designing your favorite crafts today. Make your first art sale online; in the long run, individuals will be keen on your work and can hardly doubt to buy it. The Cricut does not make you any less creative; it just makes the process easier and efforts on more important things or personalizing the projects after making the cuts. It takes the tedious work out of your hands and makes everything fun, easy, and fast.

Cricut machines are awesome gadgets to own because they do not only boost creativity and productivity. They can also be used to create crafts for business. With Design Space, crafters can create almost anything and even customize their products to bear their imprints.

You will have to practice, follow the guide I have given, and add or scratch ideas out until you have your own. All over the world, people use these machines to make gift items, t-shirts, interior décor, and many other crafts, to beautify their homes, share with friends and family during holidays, and even sell, etc.

One of the greatest things about a Cricut is that it is extremely simple to use. It does take a while to get used to using it, but once you get the hang of it, only your creativity is the limit. With that in mind, this part focuses on giving you a beginner's guide on using the Cricut. These don't look like a lot of things, but they are all the right ones to get you started. For a beginner, it is recommended that you purchase a starter set that includes the necessary accessories.

When you purchase your Cricut machine, you will be excited to get started. Search the online Cricut library for ideas on how to create cool projects that will make your environment more enjoyable, as well as projects that you can use to give others joy in their life such as cards and wooden signs.

The great thing about the Cricut is that you can use it with so many different materials that you will never run out of ideas for crafting and creating beautiful gifts. Perhaps website composition isn't for you; however, this is only one model. You can likewise make your craftsmanship accessible in prints, shirts, scratchpads, and so on. You can go to the visual communication course and produce work of art for gatherings or organizations.

Enjoy your new knowledge of your fantastic machine and give a new project a try. If you are about to start your first project, consider trying one of the beginner projects outlined. For those that have a few cuts under their belt, give one of the alternative projects a try! Have fun, and do not limit yourself. The beauty of the Cricut is the versatility of functions and user-friendly format. Use this to make your life and home and those of your friends and family more exciting and designed!

All that is needed is a couple of provisions and some simple guidelines, and you can influence everything; without exception, you can also foresee. You don't need to be a specialist, and you don't need to be great at makes. Give the Cricut a chance to do the diligent work for you, and then love the outcomes!

All the best!

Made in the USA
Las Vegas, NV
09 November 2023

80494115R00144